A Hymn for
Eternity

A Hymn for
Eternity

THE STORY OF
WALLACE HARTLEY
TITANIC
BANDMASTER

YVONNE CARROLL

The
History
Press

Frontispiece: Not one of the bandsmen on *Titanic* survived the sinking. Broadsheet published by Amalgamated Musician's Union. (Musician's Union)

Back cover image: A rare view of the *Titanic* passing Hythe pier sailing down from Southampton. This was one of the last glimpses of the ship. (By courtesy of the Univerity of Liverpool Library, D.175/2)

First published 2002
This edition 2011
Reprinted 2012

The History Press
The Mill, Brimscombe Port
Stroud, Gloucestershire, GL5 2QG
www.thehistorypress.co.uk

British Library Cataloguing in Publication Data.
A catalogue record for this book is available from the British Library.

ISBN 978 0 7524 6073 4

Typesetting and origination by The History Press
Printed in Great Britain

Contents

This book is dedicated to my mother,
Katie Eileen Carroll, 1916–2011,

The book is also dedicated to the late Jean Elizabeth Martin,
who was devoted to keeping the memory of
Wallace Hartley and the other bandsmen alive.

Acknowledgements

I 'd like to thank the many people who helped me with this project:
Various libraries throughout the North of England, with a
special mention for the staff of Rawtenstall Library; my friend
Andrea Whitehouse for invaluable help with research at the Public
Record Office, Kew; Mrs D. Stevens, a relative of Wallace Hartley, for
receiving me into her home; Garry Shutlak, Nova Scotia Archives,
Halifax; Michelle Lefevre, Leeds Library and Information Services;
Katie Hooper, University of Liverpool Special Collections (Cunard
Archives); Terence Kiernam, architect of Ripon, for information
re the building that was Collinson's Café, Victoria Quarter, Leeds;
Richard Taylor, department of listed buildings, Leeds, for information
re the Victoria Quarter, Leeds; Christine Bryant for help with the
1881 census; my husband, Chris Speak, for photographs, support, for
accompanying me on countless research expeditions and for coming
up with a title for the book.

For help with the second edition: Darran Ward for interesting
discussions and for allowing me to publish items from his collection;
Jenny O'Hara McRandall, manageress of Jigsaw, Leeds, for allowing
me to use one of her pictures of the interior of the shop that used to
be Collinson's Café; and Steve Charldwood.

My sincere apologies if I have inadvertently missed someone.

Preface

Wallace Hartley and his fellow musicians gained international fame almost overnight as news of their heroic deed made headlines around the world. Wallace was not a public figure and was relatively unknown until his death. Nor was he even a householder. It has been necessary, therefore, to trace his and his family's movements through his father, Albion.

With regard to Wallace Hartley's musical career, we know the main stages, but not necessarily the correct order. At times, therefore, in the absence of definite dates and facts, I have had to do some educated guesswork. Since the first edition was written, a few more facts have come to light and some errors have been amended. However, there are still some pieces of the jigsaw missing, or possibly in the wrong place. I trust I have made it adequately clear when I am making assumptions and when I am portraying fact, and hope I have done justice to Wallace Hartley.

Prologue

T he four colossal funnels of the *Titanic* stood out, black and ochre, against the April sky above Southampton. The black gang and other members of the crew, with their kits slung over their shoulders, were streaming down towards the ship. Passengers were gathering on the White Star dock, and excitement began to mount. But the real rush would start when the boat trains arrived from Waterloo.

Wallace Hartley was also making his way to the ship. In the last few hours, since leaving Liverpool, he had had time to ponder over his decision. He had not wanted to be bandmaster on the *Titanic*. She might be the largest and most luxurious vessel afloat, and this was her maiden voyage, but he had been happy enough on the *Mauretania*. He had only just arrived back from New York the day before, and it all seemed 'a bit of a rush'. So, of course, he would have preferred to go straight home to his parents in Yorkshire. And then there was Maria ... Maria, who was soon to be his wife.

Wallace loved the sea, and had already crossed the Atlantic eighty times on various liners as a member of the ship's orchestra, but he was thirty-three now and, in a few months' time, he was going to give it up and settle down.

Anyway, it was too late now. He had allowed himself to be persuaded and there was no going back. He had managed to send a letter home; the *Titanic* was due back in Southampton on the 27th, so he would be home in Yorkshire on the Sunday ...

1

Bonnie Colne
Upon the Hill

Bonnie Colne, Bonnie Colne.
Bonnie Colne, let come what will,
Tha'lt ever be most dear to me
Bonnie Colne upon the Hill.[1]

Wallace Hartley was not a Yorkshireman. He was born across the border in the hill town of Colne, in Lancashire, on 2 June 1878. Wallace was born in the family home at 92 Greenfield Hill,[2] one in a row of six cottages that still stand in isolation, just outside the built-up area of Colne.

Colne is in the northern part of East Lancashire, on the border with West Yorkshire, approximately thirty miles north of Manchester. It was built on Colne Water, which runs into the River Calder. Situated in the Pennines, it is surrounded by hills and moorland. Looming up a few miles to the south-west of the town is Pendle Hill, of 'Lancashire Witches' fame.[3]

The area where Colne is situated is formed from a type of sandstone called millstone grit, which forms prominent hills with valleys in between. Colne itself is situated on such a hill that stands 623ft above the surrounding countryside, with valleys to the north and south.

From a medieval market town, Colne became a centre for the woollen industry, and three-storey handloom weavers' cottages sprang up. Elizabeth Hartley, Wallace's mother, was herself a worsted weaver. John Wesley had visited the town in 1759 and had this to report: 'We went to Colne, situated on the top of a high, round hill … the drunken mob of this town used to be the terror of all the county.'

From the early nineteenth century onwards, Colne became a servant of King Cotton. Around the time Wallace Hartley was born, the nearby town of Burnley, with its 50,000 looms, produced more woven cotton than any other town in the world. It was said that, in the heyday of the cotton industry, 'The world hangs on Lancashire thread.'

Wallace's father was himself employed in the cotton industry and, at the age of twenty, he was a sizer. For some, if not all his time spent in the industry, he probably worked at Greenfield Mill, which stood on Colne Water. The main river of Colne, although little more than a stream, it ran just below the row of cottages where Wallace's family lived, the mill itself being about a hundred yards downstream. The mill was the property of John Catlow, cotton spinner.

Albion Hartley had married Elizabeth Foulds, in September 1874, at St John the Evangelist Church, Great Marsden.[4] Albion was twenty-four years old and Elizabeth twenty-three. One of the witnesses was unable to sign the register and instead made her mark, not an unusual occurrence at a time when education was not compulsory and there was still a good deal of illiteracy.

Both bride and groom came from families who were employed in the textile industry: Albion's father, Henry, by this time deceased, had been a weaver, and Robert Foulds, the bride's father, was an overlooker. Albion himself was making headway in the industry and was now an overlooker. Albion did not move far when he married, as his family's address was Greenfield Hill (later Greenfield Road). The Foulds family lived at Primrose Bank. Albion and Elizabeth both came from fairly large families, as was usual at the time. Wallace had five uncles and aunts on his father's side alone: Martha, John Rushton, Ellen, Margaret and Henry. Grandmother Mary Hartley was a dressmaker.

The day on which Wallace Hartley was born was also the anniversary of the Sunday school attached to the Bethel Independent Methodist Chapel, where his father was choirmaster. The doctor in attendance said jokingly that he would give five shillings to the collection if, at the anniversary service, they would sing *Unto Us a Child is Given*. Albion Hartley replied, 'Let me have your five shillings. We have been rehearsing it and will sing it today.'

Bethel Chapel would continue to play an important part in the life of the family, and we will return to it later in the story. While choirmaster at the chapel, a role he performed for twenty-five years,

Albion Hartley introduced and popularised the hymn *Nearer, My God, to Thee.*

Mr Hartley had to travel to Burnley to register the birth, which he did in July. He named his son Wallace Henry, the second name after his own father. The name Hartley was very common in Colne, and at one time there were Hartleys living on more than eighty streets in the town.[5] Moreover, many, if not most, of the Hartleys on the Civil Register were from this area.

Wallace was not the first child born to Albion and Elizabeth Hartley: a daughter, Mary Ellen, had been born the previous year. According to the 1881 census, Elizabeth Hartley stated her profession as a worsted weaver, but, with two small children, she may have given up work temporarily, or perhaps she just ran a few looms. Certainly, by 1891, with an even larger family, she was no longer working outside the home.

What was it like living in Colne in the late Victorian period? The Industrial Revolution had wrought great changes, but not always for the better. Handlooms had been replaced by labour-saving machinery. Spinners and weavers no longer worked in their own cottages but in huge mills. The cotton industry engendered vast wealth, but only the mill-owners became wealthy, or benefited in any way.

King Cotton ruled supreme, and by-products of this industrial and social change were the slum dwellings and generally poor, less than salubrious, living conditions of the masses. The poorest conditions were in the area of the town where most of the industry was concentrated, down by the river. Here there was back-to-back housing, as in so many industrial towns of the North. The population of the town was rapidly increasing; from approximately 8,000 in 1861, by 1911 it would be at its peak with 25,000 inhabitants. This huge influx of people could only cause enormous housing problems and overcrowding.

In the 1860s, there had been an eleven-month cotton strike bringing hundreds of weavers to the brink of starvation and also a cotton famine due to the American Civil War, when supplies of the raw material were cut off. Although Wallace Hartley was not born at the time, his parents were residents, and were probably just entering the workforce, but it is not known if or how they were affected by this hardship. By the end of the nineteenth century, conditions were generally improving: the work was better paid and the hours shorter (only fifty-six and a half hours per week!).

Most of the buildings in this area of Lancashire, even the lowliest dwellings, used to be made of the local sand-coloured millstone grit. In those far-off days before the introduction of anti-pollution laws, the air was laden with smoke and tiny particles of soot, or smuts, that came belching out of factory chimneys from the coal-powered steam engines. This smoke-laden air left its mark on buildings and found its way into people's lungs. This was certainly a very unhealthy environment, which caused various chest ailments. The buildings soon lost their golden colour, and became dark and ugly. These grim, blackened factories, with their chimneys reaching skywards, became associated with northern mill towns and gave rise to the phrase 'dark, Satanic mills' from William Blake's hymn *Jerusalem*.[6]

There was no sanitation in the town. Houses did not have water closets but 'privies', many households having to share with other tenants. The privies had to be emptied by shovel, and the 'night soil' cart would come around and collect the contents, which were then spread on fields, unless there was an epidemic in the town. Epidemics of various diseases were not uncommon, given the lack of sanitation, and typhoid broke out in the late 1870s. The usual remedies were fumigation and white-washing, and a Nuisance Inspector reported cases of disease. In 1875, a few years before Wallace Hartley was born, a local board was formed in Colne, empowered to levy rates in order to improve conditions in the town in line with the Public Health Act of the same year. The resulting sewage works were completed in 1885 and were situated on land just below the Hartley home at Greenfield Road, on the other side of the river, the land having been bought from the mill owner.

The Hartley family were fortunate enough to live well away from the slum areas of the town. Although there was a mill behind their house and Greenfield Mill not far, there were plenty of fields and open spaces for a small boy to play in.[7] The family home was typical of many dwellings built in this period, comprising a parlour at the front of the house, a living room at the back and a small, 'lean-to' kitchen. Upstairs were two bedrooms and an attic. In front of the house there was, and still is, a small garden, an advantage that most of the terraced houses of the time did not enjoy. To the rear of the house was the usual backyard, which, in those days, would contain the privy.

Those of us whose parents or grandparents were contemporaries of Wallace Hartley are familiar with such local delicacies as black pudding (served from huge vats on outdoor markets), cow heel, tripe and elder (cow's udder), sheep's head (not enjoyed by everyone!), bread and dripping. There is no evidence to show that any of these dishes were served in the Hartley household, but Wallace would certainly be familiar with them as part of the local fayre. As a matter of interest, the first fish and chip shop inland opened in Colne in 1880.

By the end of the century, more children were being educated, as the rising number of schools shows. At first, all education was provided by church schools, built by voluntary subscription and the occasional government grant, and run by the churches concerned. A Wesleyan Sunday school opened on Great George Street in the centre of the town in 1869, and it became a day school ten years later. A number of wealthy Methodists, notably cotton manufacturers, donated sums of money to fund the building of the school. Tablets of stone with the names of the benefactors form a frieze along the front of the building. This is the school which, as a Methodist, Wallace Hartley attended. Education was not free: parents were charged a small fee, which varied according to their earnings. The Three Rs were taught in the school. A native of Colne, who attended the school in the 1950s, remembers that the interior of the building was very handsome with large quantities of oak in evidence.

The headmaster at George Street Wesleyan was Mr Thomas Baldwin, who would remain there throughout Wallace's school career. In charge of the infants when Wallace began school was Miss Etherington, replaced not long after by Miss Kezia Whittam. Wallace would have had to walk about one mile to reach the school, which was 'up town'. From his house he would have walked along Greenfield Road, which joined the main road at the bottom of Primet Hill, up the hill past the railway station, carrying on up Albert Road, and, when he reached the top of the hill, he would turn right into Exchange Street, where the main entrance to the school was situated.

The Education Act of 1870 allowed for schools to be created by elected School Boards with powers to charge fees and accept government grants. Local church schools were fiercely opposed to Board schools, and local people feared a rise in rates to fund them. Consequently, a School Board was not set up in Colne until 1896, by which time Wallace Hartley had completed his education.

By 1881, Wallace's father had been made mill manager. He had worked his way to the top, and owed his success to his sound financial sense and skills for leadership, qualities that would stand him in good stead when embarking on a career change that was soon to take place.

A dramatic episode in the lives of the Hartley family occurred in February 1885. On the morning of Sunday the 1st, fire broke out at Greenfield Mill. The fire started in the new section of the building, which was three storeys high with attic rooms above, and eight windows long. The building contained 15,000 spindles. The damage caused amounted to approximately £10,000, but fortunately no one was hurt, and the fire led to the formation of Colne's Volunteer Fire Brigade. The most important outcome of the event was the fact that 120 lost their livelihoods, including, presumably, Wallace's father.

Albion Hartley was therefore obliged to seek alternative employment, and he became an agent with the Refuge Assurance Company, whose headquarters for the Colne and Nelson district were based on Manchester Road in the centre of Nelson, approximately two miles from where the family lived.[8]

Another direct consequence of the fire and change of employment was that the family moved from their cottage in Greenfield Road to a slightly larger house at 1 Burnley Road, at the foot of Primet Hill. This was near the site of Primrose Bank, where Wallace's mother had lived as a girl. The house was at the end of a short block; next door was (and still is) a post office and, at the other end, stands a public house called The Queen's. About 100 yards up the hill was the railway station, which was convenient, as Albion Hartley may have used the railway to travel the two miles to his new job in Nelson; the tram service between the two towns would not start until 1903. Another advantage of living here was that Wallace would not have so far to walk to school, as his journey had been practically halved.

Towards the end of 1885, when Wallace was seven years old, a brother, Ughtred Harold, was born. This unusual name is not unique to the Hartley family, as a prominent citizen of the town shared the same name. Unfortunately, tragedy struck a little more than a year later, when, at the beginning of 1887, the little boy died. Infant mortality, although on the decrease, was still high, and family historians will agree that most families lost at least one child, usually under the age of five, to one of of the many diseases that were rife at the time: diphtheria, meningitis, scarlet fever, and the odd outbreak of typhoid. Wallace's brother died of scarlatina and was buried in the local cemetery on Keighley Road at the other end of town.

Around the time of Ughtred's death, another daughter was born to the Hartley family. She was named Elizabeth after her mother, but would be known as Lizzie. Her exact date of birth is not known, as two children of the same name were registered in Burnley in that period: one being born in the third quarter of 1886, the other the first quarter of 1887, which is when her brother died. Elizabeth was four years old at the time of the 1891 census.

Wallace's school days were remembered by another pupil at the school, Mr Tom Hyde, who, as an old man in the mid-1950s (at the time the film *A Night to Remember* came to the screens), recalled:

I was at George Street Wesleyan School with him, though he was at a higher standard than me. I found him all right. He seemed a very nice lad, a bit what you might call roughish – a big tomboy. But he was very smart-looking, a lad with a sense of fun. We all started learning music and the violin together in the bottom classroom at George Street. There would be about twenty of us, and we were all about eleven or twelve years old. I don't remember that Wallace was any different from any of us in his violin playing, but he seemed to come on remarkably afterwards. I also used to go swimming with him, and we went to the baths once a week. He was a jolly good swimmer

Mrs Hyde also remembered Wallace, as the Hartley family home at 1 Burnley Road is near Knott's Lane, where she lived as a girl. The journey from Colne to Albion Hartley's new place of work must have proved arduous as, in 1888, the family moved to Nelson and took up residence at 13 Carr Road, a handsome terrace near the centre of town. We must assume that Wallace and his sister had to transfer temporarily to another school, but we have no record of this.

In the summer of 1889, a new brother arrived for Wallace, Mary Ellen and Elizabeth. Conrad Robert was Albion and Elizabeth's third son, but, alas, he was to share the same fate as his brother Ughtred, and died in the spring of 1891, aged one year and several months. He was the second son that his parents had to bury: Conrad Robert joined his infant brother in Colne Cemetery.

For much of their childhood, and certainly their formative years, Wallace and his sister Mary were the only children in the Hartley household. Because of the rather isolated location of their Greenfield Hill home, they may have had few other companions outside school hours. Even when the other children came along, the age gap was so great that Wallace and Mary probably continued to spend a great deal of time in each other's company. Music would become another bond between them. They grew so close, in fact, that Mary would later call her first child after her brother.

There is a school photograph in a private collection showing Wallace aged about fourteen, with approximately fifteen other boys and their teacher. These were probably the school-leavers for that year, and were from families who could afford to continue sending them to school as opposed to sending them out to work in a local mill to augment the family income. This was the fate of most working-class children, as attendance at school was compulsory only until the age of ten. Some of the boys in the picture were wearing fob watches, an indicator of their family's relative affluence. In 1895 there were three outbreaks of infectious diseases at the school, but, fortunately for Wallace, he had already left the school. By 1899 it would be the largest school in Colne with 624 pupils.

Wallace's violin playing certainly was 'coming on' and he later joined the Colne Orchestral Society, which was founded in 1892 by J. Lascelles-Wildman. The first concert was held in the Cloth Hall. Wallace was also a chorister at Bethel Chapel, where his father was choirmaster. There were instrument dealers and private music teachers in the town, and Wallace continued to have music tuition after he left school, as we are told that his father 'placed him under capable instructors'. One of these was Mr Pickles Riley of Bridge Street in the town. He was not a professional music teacher, but was an overlooker, and later manager, in the textile industry. He was probably chosen because of his connection with Bethel Chapel.

Wallace's father, however, did not wish his son to embark on a musical career. On leaving school, therefore, Wallace went to work at the Union Bank, which was situated at 17 Albert Road. It is highly probable that the position was found for Wallace by his father, who was keen that he should start a career in commerce. As a bank clerk, Wallace 'gave every satisfaction, for he was steady, attentive and capable'.

While out and about in town, Wallace was able to observe the progress being made on the new Town Hall building. With its tall clock tower, it became the highest building in Colne, and, situated at the very top of the hill, is still a landmark that can be seen from far and wide.[9]

Some years later, a Mr Edward Johnson, from Yorkshire, recalled that Wallace, while in his teens, had travelled over with his parents and sister, Mary, to the Wesleyan School, Savile Town, Dewsbury, to perform at a concert given there. His sister 'sang very beautifully' and Wallace 'delighted everyone with his playing of the violin'. Wallace was described as a 'grand lad', which is the highest praise, in North Country terms, for a boy or young man.

Albion Hartley was being quickly promoted in the insurance business. In 1890 he had become assistant superintendent with the Refuge. This promotion enabled the family to move up the hill onto Albert Road, which had become the main residential area in the town. The Hartleys moved into No.90, which was situated in a block of three houses attached to the Crown Hotel, just above the railway station.

The last surviving child born to the Hartleys was Hilda. In all likelihood, she was born in 1894, as, although two baby girls of that name were registered that year in Burnley, there were no others in the previous or subsequent years. By this time, Albion and Elizabeth had been married for twenty years. Wallace was therefore brought up surrounded by three sisters, but he was not spoilt. His father would later say that Wallace was 'an ideal son' who never spoke an unkind word to his parents or the members of his family and 'never caused his father or mother a single moment's trouble.' One can imagine that Albion and Elizabeth Hartley cherished their only surviving son, and, at times, must have feared losing him, too.

By 1893, Albion had become superintendent at the Refuge, and, two years later, he was moved to Huddersfield to pursue his career. Thus began the family's residence in Yorkshire. Wallace Hartley was seventeen years old.

Endnotes

1   Colne's anthem, composed by Frank Slater.
2   Now Greenfield Road.
3   The supposed witches, among whom were Dame Demdike and Old Chattox, lived in the hamlets and countryside near the foot of the hill in the seventeenth century, when witch hunts were rife. They were taken to Lancaster jail, tried and publicly hanged in 1612. Books on the subject include *Mist over Pendle* and *Lancashire Witches*. The hill is also famous among Quakers as being the site where George Fox, founder of the Quaker religion, had his first 'vision'. There is a Quaker building in Pennsylvania called Pendle House.
4   This is the town which is now called Nelson and is situated between Burnley and Colne, the boundary being very close to where Wallace was born.

5   William Pickles Hartley, the jam manufacturer, was a native of Colne, but was
    no relation.
6   These conditions prevailed until the introduction of anti-pollution legislation
    and 'smoke-free' zones in the late 1960s.
7   Behind the row of houses is a field where a corn mill once stood. The M65
    motorway runs along the perimeter of the field and comes to an end at a
    roundabout at the corner of the same field. The back of the row of houses
    can be seen from the motorway, which is less than 100m away.
8   The branch closed down and has now been replaced by another business, but,
    until recently, the faint lettering REFUGE ASSURANCE CO. could still be
    read on the front of the building.
9   The architect was Alfred Waterhouse, who also designed the magnificent
    Town Hall in Manchester, both buildings sharing the same pseudo-gothic
    style. It was opened on 13 January 1894, and Colne gained borough status in
    1895.

2

The Yorkshire Connection

Colne had nurtured the young Wallace Hartley, but it was in Yorkshire that he would flourish as a musician and where he would spend his adult life.

Albion Hartley's promotion took the family to the much larger town of Huddersfield in the West Riding. The family took up residence at 35 Somerset Road, in the Almondbury area of the town, just off the Wakefield road. At least we must presume that they moved straight into this address, there being no records for the period 1895–1897. They were definitely here in 1897, and it is hardly likely that they moved house twice within a two-year period.

Somerset Road is in a leafy residential area, and the block where the Hartley family lived is composed of large terraced houses. No.35 is a very handsome three-storey house with a gable roof. To the front is a small garden surrounded by a high railing.[1] Directly opposite is a golf course concealed by woodland. For the Hartley family, this was a definite step up the property ladder. A tramway ran along Somerset Road, which could take them the short distance to the town centre: down onto the Wakefield road (then called Storths), over Somerset Bridge which spans the River Calder, and up into the town.

By 1899, the Refuge Co. had premises on a prime location site in the town centre at 28 Ramsden Street,[2] across from the Town Hall, and a few doors away from the building that is now the library. However, in records for 1897, when the Hartleys had already left Colne, the Refuge did not appear on a list of insurance brokers for the town, and the premises at Ramsden Street were vacant (there was a surgeon at No.26). Albion Hartley was listed as superintendent in 1901, and had probably fulfilled this capacity since his arrival in the town.

For this early period in Yorkshire, there is no reference anywhere regarding Wallace. Although becoming more proficient as a musician, it would be some years before his life would take a different direction. In the meantime, he continued life as a clerk. His father would no doubt have been instrumental in finding him a new situation. Albion himself was a freemason and would have had numerous contacts in the world of business and finance.

While in Huddersfield, Wallace became a member of the Philharmonic Orchestra. In 1895, the year the Hartley family moved to Yorkshire, the orchestra had seventy musicians. At the time, subscription concerts were held in the Town Hall at Huddersfield, and the Philharmonic Orchestra performed under the baton of Mr J.E. Ibeson, often accompanying well-known soloists of the day. Tickets for the concerts cost one shilling.

On Tuesday 6 October 1896, the second part of the concert consisted of Gounod's opera, *Philemon and Baucis*. The role of Baucis, a 'poor peasant woman', was played by Madame Fanny Moody, and the part of Jupiter was played by Mr Charles Manners. Wallace may have been playing in the orchestra that evening. Certainly, in later years, these two singers would play a significant role in the life of Wallace Hartley.

While Wallace was developing as a violinist, his elder sister, Mary, was a talented singer. We know that, while living in Colne, she and Wallace had once travelled to Saviletown near Dewsbury with their parents to perform in a concert. Mary was now a well-known soloist in a Milnsbridge church choir. In the summer of 1897, there was cause for celebration in the Hartley household. Mary, now twenty years old, married Thomas Ernest Sellers in Huddersfield. One can imagine a huge family reunion with numerous relatives arriving from Colne. Two years later, a baby was born: George Wallace.[3]

Wallace was now in his twenties, and had not yet embarked on a musical career. However, that was soon to change. As Wallace's love of the violin grew, he wanted increasingly to become a professional violinist, and he found his work as a clerk 'irksome'. Although his father did not want him to pursue a career in music, and was no doubt of the opinion that commerce was a safer option, he eventually relented. Both he and Wallace's mother felt at some point that it was inevitable.

By 1901, Wallace had fulfilled his dream and was now a professional musician, but the early stages of his career are still unclear. We know many events in his musical career, but not always the precise order in which they occurred. When the census was taken in April 1901, Wallace was almost certainly touring, or had recently been touring, in a musical capacity, as there was a young man from the South of England staying as a visitor in the Hartley household. Like Wallace, Herbert W. Stubley was twenty-two years old, and he, too, was a musician. In all probability Wallace had joined the Moody-Manners Opera Company, formed by Fanny Moody and Charles Manners, who had sung in Huddersfield a few years previously and had undoubtedly made an impression on the young Wallace. This may have been the reason why, in December 1898, Wallace received the following letter from Mr A.C. Whitehead, Assistant Honorary Secretary of the Huddersfield Philharmonic Orchestra:

> *Dear Sir,*
> *The committee of the Philharmonic Society*
> *wish to know if they can rely on your*
> *attendance at the rehearsals and concerts in future.*
>   *Yours etc*

Was Wallace no longer in Huddersfield and had he thrown his lot in with Fanny Moody and Charles Manners?[11]

Fanny Moody had made her stage debut in Liverpool with the Carl Rosa Company, and remained their leading soprano until 1898. She was said to have a light soprano voice and her charming stage personality was much admired. Charles Manners, too, was a member of the Carl Rosa Company, and toured with them from 1882 until 1890. In that year he married Fanny Moody. He then went on to sing at Covent Garden and in the United States.

In 1898, the Moody-Manners Company was formed to promote grand opera in English. Along with Carl Rosa, they were to be the principal training ground for opera singers before the First World War. They made a modest start, touring the provinces, but, by 1902, they had two companies: the principal company with 175 members, doing seasons in London, and a smaller one consisting of ninety-five members, that did most of the touring. They had seasons at Covent Garden, Drury Lane and other London theatres, but their dream of founding a National Opera Company centred in London was never realised, and Moody-Manners gave its last performance in 1916.

According to a fellow violinist in the Huddersfield Philharmonic Orchestra, Mr Arthur Armitage, the Hartley family lived for three years in the village of Linthwaite, just outside Huddersfield. The family was still at Somerset Road in the early part of 1902, but, in the second half of that year, the house was unoccupied. In fact, they can be traced to the Cowlersley Lane area of Milnsbridge, a small township situated a couple of miles outside Huddersfield on the road to Manchester. For the year 1904, the address for Albion Hartley was given in a local directory as Storth, a very small area situated just below the boundary with Linthwaite. The lane runs up quite a steep hill, and Storth is approximately three quarters of a mile from the main Huddersfield–Manchester road. A housing estate exists here now, but old maps show that a few fairly large houses had previously stood here and were demolished in the 1930s. In all likelihood it is here that the Hartley family lived in pleasant surroundings, far from the grimy town centre of Huddersfield.

In the spring of 1903, it came to Wallace's attention that they were short of a violinist for the start of the season in the Bridlington Municipal Orchestra, so, in May of that year, Wallace took himself to the East Riding resort, where he was to become first violin.

The Municipal Orchestra had started life as the Sea Wall Band. The band played on the north promenade that had been known as the Sea Wall Parade, before being renamed the Royal Prince's Parade in 1888: 'a charming marine parade' that was considered to be the resort's finest asset. At first the musicians did not even have a bandstand, but this situation was remedied in the late 1800s. The band became the Municipal Orchestra when Bridlington became a borough in 1899.

The band also had a new conductor for the 1903 season: Herr Sigmund Winternitz, a jovial-looking man with a huge handlebar moustache. Because of Herr Winternitz's Austrian origins, the band was known as the Royal Viennese Band, and performed in military-style uniforms.

The Royal Viennese Band was 'a brilliant success'; indeed, it was 'the most popular the Parade ever had'. However, the bandstand was open to the elements, and, in the 1903 season, there were more rainy days than fine ones, with the result that the musicians and vocalists at times had to perform in very difficult conditions. The public, with no shelter, could not stand and listen in the pouring rain.

The Corporation, therefore, decided to act: they engaged the services of Messrs Magnall & Littlewood, architects, who had the task of designing a structure that would fit the limited space available on the Parade. The resulting pavilion, built chiefly of iron and glass, was 133ft long and 60ft wide, and could accommodate 1,700 people sitting and standing. The roof was supported by ornamental pillars and the front was open with steps leading down to the promenade. The bandstand was incorporated into this structure. The new pavilion, which had cost £2,300, was ready for the start of the 1904 season. It would become known as the Floral Pavilion, because the interior was decorated with scores of hanging-baskets suspended from the ceiling with flowers cascading all around.

The season began at Whitsuntide and the first concert was on Thursday 19 May. There was no formal opening of the new pavilion, although one or two worthy councillors were said to have brought speeches in their pockets, but 'mercifully spared the audience', who preferred to listen to Herr Winternitz's 'excellent band'. The band performed two programmes, which were 'well received and frequently applauded'. The acoustics of the new pavilion were said to be 'really splendid'.

For the rest of the season the band would perform twice daily, in the morning from 11.00a.m. until 1.00p.m. and in the evening from 7.30p.m. to 9.30p.m. On Sundays, there would be a grand sacred concert at 8.00p.m. Empire Day in 1904 fell on 24 May, and, to mark the occasion, there was a special programme of 'national and patriotic vocal and instrumental music.' The vocalist for the first week of the season was Miss Mabel Manson, a soprano from New Zealand.

Wallace Hartley can be seen in a contemporary monochrome photograph taken in the Floral Pavilion, with the windows of the bandstand in the background.[4] The orchestra and conductor are wearing their military-style uniforms, which were probably red.[5] Wallace, as first violin, can be seen on the front row just to the left of the conductor. Later photographs taken inside the pavilion show the orchestra wearing black suits. In all likelihood, the photograph was taken to mark the opening of the pavilion.

In Bridlington, Wallace must have stayed in lodgings, as he could not travel daily from Huddersfield. In 1905, Wallace's family moved from Huddersfield, as Mr Hartley's job took him to Leeds. By coincidence, the premises of the Refuge Co. in Leeds were on Albion Street, at No.3. This street runs between Boar Lane and the Headrow, both main thoroughfares through the centre of the city. The location of No.3 is now part of a modern shopping precinct.

Wallace was now twenty-seven years old and keen to further his musical career. With his family settled in the expanding and prosperous city of Leeds, it was time for a move that would allow him to live with his family and work closer to home.

We know that Wallace Hartley played at the Kursaal in Harrogate, but the Kursaal did not open until 1903, when Wallace was in Bridlington. Harrogate at the time was a very fashionable spa town, and the Kursaal was built as 'an act of faith in the future of the town', with the aim of providing 'a first-class place for high-class entertainment'. Building began in January 1902, using plans by architect R.J. Beale. Later on in the project, the plans would be enhanced by Frank Matchem of London, who was considered to be a brilliant architect and one of the very greatest designers of theatres.[6] He designed the London Coliseum and would later redesign the London Palladium. The Harrogate Kursaal is a rare example of a building that was designed on the lines of the German kursaals, having a level, rather than sloping, floor, and a series of encircling promenades.

Two concerts were held to mark the opening of this magnificent building, the first one on Wednesday 27 May 1903. Sir Hubert Parry, Bart., performed the opening ceremony, which was followed by 'a grand ballad and orchestral concert'. The main performer was Miss Marie Hall, who was a solo violinist. The singers were accompanied by the fifty-strong Municipal Orchestra.

The Municipal Orchestra would go on to perform at the Kursaal every day except Sunday; there were morning, afternoon and evening concerts. Local bands also appeared, such as the Temperance Band, the Irish Guards and the Harrogate Volunteers' Band. Many famous soloists and conductors performed at the Kursaal, including Pavlova, Dame Nellie Melba and Sir Edward Elgar.[7] On 16 July 1904, Sarah Bernhardt appeared here in *La Dame aux Camélias*, one of her most famous roles. In September 1904, for one week, the Carl Rosa Opera Company, billed as 'the oldest opera company in the world', gave an operatic festival, including *Carmen*, *Don Giovanni* and *Faust*. At a later point in Wallace's career, this opera company would offer him the opportunity to spread his wings.

The names of the musicians in the Municipal Orchestra, as well as any solo performers, were printed in weekly programmes for the Kursaal. Unfortunately the programmes are missing for the crucial years 1905–1908, so it is impossible to know exactly when Wallace took up his position with the orchestra, whether in 1905 or at a later date, but he definitely did not spend more than two seasons in Bridlington.

ST. GEORGE'S HALL,
BRADFORD.

WEDNESDAY, DECEMBER 26th, 1900,

FOR FOUR NIGHTS AND TWO MATINEES.

Special Morning Performances, Boxing Day, Dec. 26th, and Saturday, December 29th.

Early Doors 1 o'clock.   Commence at 2 prompt.

THE WORLD-RENOWNED ROYAL

CARL ROSA OPERA COMPANY

Under the Direction of Mr. T. H. FRIEND

The Carl Rosa CHORUS & ORCHESTRA

(OF PROFESSIONAL OPERATIC ARTISTES).

Conductors	-	Mr. EUGENE GOOSSENS and Mr. WALTER VAN NOORDEN
Leader and Assistant Conductor	...	Mr ISIDORE SCHWILLER
Stage Manager	...	Mr. G. BEALE
Advance Representative	...	Mr. ARTHUR H. YOLLAND

Willsons', Printers, Leicester.

Programme of the Carl Rosa Opera Company. (From the collection of the late Jean Elizabeth Martin)

We are told that Wallace played engagements in and around Leeds while he was 'at the Kursaal', as and when the opportunity arose. He played for a time at the mansion in Roundhay Park, the municipal park on the outskirts of the city. Once the home of the Nicholson family, the mansion and park were bought by the council and leased for use as a hotel, which provided catering for various functions. Although there was a bandstand located close to the mansion, it is more likely that Wallace played as part of a café-style orchestra to

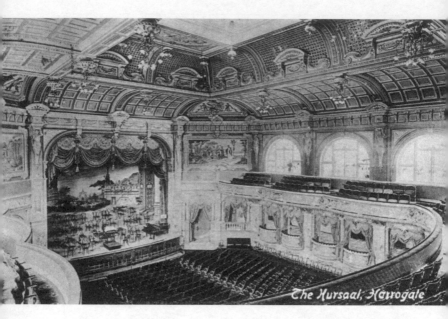

Interior of the Kursaal. Built on the German model, it had an encircling promenade. (From the collection of the late Jean Elizabeth Martin)

entertain diners. During this time, Wallace was gaining experience and establishing himself as a musician.

In Leeds, the family's address was 48 Hillcrest Avenue, which is now part of the inner-city area of Chapeltown, but, in 1905, this was a middle-class area on the very outskirts of the city. The avenue of terraced houses had only recently been built as part of a building boom, on what had previously been open pastureland, beyond the suburb of New Leeds, which was an affluent residential area. The avenue ran parallel with Spencer Place at right angles to Cowper Street. The house was smaller and less handsome than the one they had left in Somerset Road, but this may have been because accommodation in the expanding city of Leeds was more expensive than in Huddersfield. Next door, at No.50, was John Moore, draper's manager, across the road was a civil engineer and further along lived the editor of the *Leeds Mercury*.

In later years, especially the 1930s, when the more affluent members of society wanted to escape the pollution and grime near city centres, they abandoned the superior terraced rows like the ones around Hillcrest Avenue, and moved even further out of the city into newly built semi-detached houses in leafy suburbs, which then became fashionable as healthier and more desirable places to live. But when the Hartley family moved into Chapeltown, they were moving into a desirable, residential area.

The centre of Leeds was undergoing great changes, brought about by the wealth engendered by the woollen industry. The city had experienced rapid expansion in the mid-nineteenth century, which led to a growth in civic pride. Leeds became a city by Royal Charter in 1893. Here it was that Michael Marks of Marks & Spencer set up a market stall in 1884, not yet selling the lingerie that would make them famous, but the needles, cotton and everything necessary for Victorian women to make their own, as most of them did.[8] A sign hung on the stall, 'Don't ask the price, it's a penny'. In 1903, shortly before the Hartley family moved to Leeds, the City Square was opened to a crowd of 100,000 people. The square is dominated by a bronze equestrian statue of the Black Prince, who points majestically towards the city centre.

A development that would have a direct impact on the life and career of Wallace Hartley was begun at the turn of the century. A large area of the city east of Briggate, the main and oldest thoroughfare in the city, was being redeveloped. The Leeds Estates Co. Ltd was responsible for this huge project, which was designed by the architect Frank Matcham of London, who was renowned for his work on theatres and had redesigned the London Palladium. Several streets between Briggate and Vicar Lane were to be demolished, and an Edwardian shopping precinct, now called the Victoria Quarter, erected on the site.

The plans were drawn up in several sections, approved by the city's planning authorities, and built in stages, the first part being completed in 1900. The resulting streets and arcades were built in red brick with terracotta coping. Around all the windows and at roof level ornate detail was added, and at the corner of each block a turret was erected. The whole complex, in its proportions, harmony and magnificence, is testimony to the wealth of the city and the Edwardian love of elegance and beauty.

Situated at the lower section of the area to be redeveloped was Cheapside, site of the old Shambles (butchers' stalls). Plans for Block D, which consisted of the area between Cheapside, Cross Arcade and

Vicar Lane, were approved in 1901, and the building was completed by 1902. This block consisted of nine shops, a warehouse and the Dolphin Hotel. Cheapside was renamed King Edward Street, which was more in keeping with the handsome buildings.

At No.23 King Edward Street, plans were submitted in March 1902 for 'tea rooms, bakery and 7 WCs'. The building work involved the extension of the premises back into the warehouse that stood in a courtyard behind the shops. This free-standing building had a glass window in the roof. As part of the grandiose extension plans, this window was replaced by a huge glass dome. The extended area was two floors high, with curving staircases leading to the upper level. Columns and archways supporting the great dome at both levels created recesses in the corners. Between the two floors was a large, elliptical well protected by a balustrade, forming a balcony, or encircling promenade. One can imagine the elegant Edwardian clients peering over, and those below looking up towards the dome, the light from which would stream down onto both floors. The whole effect was one of beauty and elegance.

According to expert opinion, the building work was probably completed one year after the plans were submitted. Originally Ashby's Café, by 1907 the tea rooms had become the Orient Café, and were owned by T. Collinson & Sons. Collinsons had been in business for fifty-seven years in other towns in Yorkshire as tea dealers and blenders, as well as coffee merchants. They also had cafés in other locations in Leeds city centre: on Albion Street (where father Albion worked for the Refuge Company) and another on Welllington Street. Collinson's Orient Café soon became a popular venue for fashionable society of the day, so much so that an orchestra was engaged to provide music for the sophisticated clientele. It is not known exactly when the orchestra was first formed, but it *is* known that Wallace Hartley became a member. Wallace may have also played at the other Collinson cafés in the city.

At the end of every October, which marked the end of the season in Harrogate, the numbers performing in the Kursaal orchestra were reduced considerably: first violins from seven to four, second violins from six to two. Wallace may have been made redundant and he probably saw his opportunity when the orchestra at Collinson's Café came into existence.

Maybe it was in Collinson's Café that Wallace met Maria Robinson. Maria was two years younger than Wallace, having been born in

---

ROYAL PRINCE'S PARADE, BRIDLINGTON.

Manager   —   Mr. CHARLES PALMER.

THE FASHIONABLE RENDEZVOUS.

E NORMOUS   W HITSUNTIDE   A TTRACTIONS !

OPENING OF THE GRAND NEW PAVILION SHELTER

ROYAL   VIENNESE   BAND

UNDER THE PERSONAL DIRECTION OF **HERR SIGMUND WINTERNITZ,**

(The Brilliant Success of Last Season).

PLAYS TWICE DAILY   —   MORNING, 11·0 to 1·0; EVENING, 7-30 to 9-30.

EXTRA PERFORMANCE WHIT-MONDAY AFTERNOON at 3-0.

GRAND SACRED CONCERTS each Sunday Evening at 8-0.

E MPIRE DAY, TUESDAY, May 24th.—SPECIAL PROGRAMME

OF NATIONAL AND PATRIOTIC VOCAL AND INSTRUMENTAL MUSIC.

Vocalist for Week:

MISS MABEL MANSON, the New Zealand Soprano.

ADMISSION.—Day Ticket, 6d.; Saturday to Monday, 1s. 3d.; Friday to Tuesday, 2s.; One Week, 2s. 6d.   Periodical and Family Tickets on issue.

Advertisement for the opening of the Floral Pavilion, Bridlington. (By courtesy of East Riding of Yorkshire Information Services)

1880 into a family of manufacturers from Leeds. Grandfather Joshua H. Robinson was a 'malterer, corn dealer and woollen manufacturer'. Her father, Benjamin Laurence Herbert, dealt with the corn milling side of operations, while his elder brother, John Herbert, worked in the maltering side of the business. As a girl, Maria lived in the Wortley area of Leeds, just south of the River Aire. The family lived at New Houses on Whitehall Road, one of the main thoroughfares into the city from a south-westerly direction. The Robinson factory was nearby at 26 Mill Green. In the 1890s, after the retirement of Maria's grandfather, the business was registered in the name of John Herbert Robinson, and the two brothers seem to have concentrated on woollen manufacturing.

By 1891, there were three more surviving children in the Robinson household: Margaret, who was a year younger than Maria, William, who was two years younger, and Mary, who was just one year old. The family were still living in the Wortley area of Leeds, although at a different address, but, at some time between 1897 and 1901, as their fortunes grew, they moved ten miles away to Boston Spa, 'a pretty watering place, situated on the River Wharfe, where there is capital boating and fishing.' Here they lived in a villa called St Ives, which had been built in 1886. Boston Spa had been superseded as a spa town by Harrogate when a local landowner refused to allow a railway to be built on his land, thus depriving the town of a station. Instead, a station was built at Thorp Arch, about a mile from Boston Spa, and an omnibus met the trains, carrying passengers back and forth. The Robinson family would later move to 'Dooklands' at Thorp Arch.

Wallace came to Boston Spa to court Maria. One of Wallace's visits was described by John H. Wood, who later married Maria's younger sister, Mary. A party of them had been boating on the river one Sunday morning, and Wallace had insisted on doing his share of the rowing on the way back. This meant rowing against the stream, after which Wallace noticed to his chagrin that blisters were beginning to appear on his hands. The next day, after playing at Collinson's, he complained that he had 'made his hands very bad for playing'.

On another occasion, the group was walking on Ingleborough and got caught in fog. John Wood said that Wallace regarded it 'with delight at the time, and with boyish pride afterwards'.

John Wood went on to say that Wallace had 'a pair of the most beautiful, slender and white hands I have ever seen on a man'. He goes on to provide the following description of Wallace: 'I seem to see him now in a characteristic attitude when seated – half reclining in an easy fashion in the armchair. Two long, white fingers of his left hand held along his chin, and two supporting his head; a long, lean face, dark brown eyes, long hair, blackish, with a rich brown lustre – not over long, but I never saw it short.' Wallace and John Wood were the same age, so they probably got on well together.

Wallace made many friends in Leeds, and became a member of the Savage Club. Founded in the 1890s by a group of artists, writers and musicians, its aims were to 'develop and foster social and congenial good fellowship, encourage good Music, Art, Literary and Kindred subjects, Walking and Camping'. They prided themselves on their Bohemian spirit, and elected as their chief one Edmund Bogg, who has been described as 'the last great Yorkshire character'.

Prospective members had to be proposed and seconded by existing members and elected by the whole membership. The eight members of the committee were known as Braves.

The meetings, or pow-wows, were usually held in Bogg's picture-framing workshop in Land's Lane. The old chief, sitting ceremoniously in his feathered head-dress, would preside over the young, and often boisterous, Savages. The members provided their own entertainment: papers were read, instruments played, songs sung. At midnight, when spirits were high after the Firewater Pot had been passed round, a vocalist would be called upon to go upstairs and sing through a hole in the floor to the assembled group below.[9]

Members of the Savage Club gave concerts periodically for various charitable causes. It was later claimed in the newspapers that the last concert in which Wallace played with the Savages was held on 26 November 1908 in aid of the National Lifeboat Saturday Fund, but, unfortunately, no programme for the concert has survived. In 1910, members of the Savage Club held a farewell dinner in honour of Edmund Bogg at Collinson's Café, but Wallace Hartley was not present. He was no longer a member of the Savage Club, nor, indeed, an employee at Collinson's. Wallace Hartley had moved on.

In 1908, there had been important changes at the Refuge in Leeds. The company moved to a new location at 23 Bond Street in the city centre. There was also a staff reshuffle and Wallace's father was moved yet again, this time to the smaller mill town of Dewsbury.

This move must have been another promotion for Albion Hartley, as the family moved into a considerably larger house called 'Surreyside' in West Park Street; very handsome houses in a quiet, residential neighbourhood.

Wallace must have missed the bustle of city life and all the social activities that the city afforded. More importantly, although Dewsbury was only a few train stops from Leeds, it would be inconvenient for Wallace to work at Collinson's. It was probably at this time, therefore, if not before, that Wallace considered a career move. As a mark of his popularity, when he left Collinson's Cafe, he was presented with a silver matchbox with the inscription: 'To W.H.H. from Collinson's Staff'.

For Wallace, the move to Dewsbury had added significance: it took him further away from Maria. However, he was not ready to settle down: he was too busy pursuing his musical career, and he would go where it would take him...

His career in music took Wallace away from Yorkshire. Good fortune would have it that he was engaged in the orchestra of the Carl Rosa Opera Company. This was a more prestigious position for a musician, and Wallace must have relished the prospect of playing in a full-size orchestra to large audiences around the country.

The company had been formed in the early 1870s, and was in its thirty-fourth consecutive season when it performed at the Kursaal,

Harrogate, in 1904. Carl Rosa had been born Karl August Nikolaus Rose in Hamburg in 1842, and studied in Leipzig, where he became friends with Arthur Sullivan. Originally a violinist, he married the famous soprano Madame Parepa in New York, and together they

Programme for a concert at Huddersfield in 1896. Wallace became a member of the Municipal Orchestra and may have been playing on this occasion. Singers Fanny Moody and Charles Manners later formed an opera company and Wallace toured with them for a while. (By courtesy of Huddersfield Public Library)

Programme for the opening of the Kursaal, Harrogate. (By courtesy of Harrogate Borough Council)

formed the Parepa-Rosa English Opera Company, Rosa himself becoming manager and conductor. In 1872, the company transferred to England.

The company never owned its own theatre, although they used the Royal Court Theatre in Liverpool as a base for a time. They had seasons in London, but their main aim was to tour the country in order to bring opera to the provinces. Their productions were always in English, and, after the collapse of the Royal English Opera House, the Carl Rosa Company was the only one in the country to produce serious operas in the vernacular.

The 1880s were the most prosperous period for the company. In 1893, after a performance at Balmoral, the company was granted the royal charter by Queen Victoria, but Rosa had died without witnessing this in 1889.

The Carl Rosa Company has a special place in the history of English opera; it was the most successful and long-lived English touring company, providing opera in the provinces for over seventy-five years. Sir Henry Wood and Sir Thomas Beecham were both conductors with the company. Eva Turner, one of the most famous singers of her day, started her career in the Carl Rosa chorus. The company has recently undergone a revival (1998), and is again a thriving touring company.[10]

One of the most important events in the history of the company was the première in England of Puccini's *La Bohème*. The composer himself came over for the first performance, which took place in Manchester on 22 April 1897. Puccini was described as 'a merry, smiling fellow, with a plentiful supply of Italian jokes, and radiant with the recollection of genuine Lancashire cheering.'

Wallace Hartley did not witness Puccini's visit, as it would be several years before he joined the company. It was later claimed that he spent three years touring with them. If this is indeed the case, then he must have joined before his family left Leeds in 1908. However, it is possible that he joined around 1908, but spent fewer than three years with them.

Wallace's travels with the company took him the length and breadth of the country. One of his associates had a photograph of him taken in Salisbury, and other acquaintances place him in Bexhill and Dover. Wallace Hartley must have thought that the world was his oyster.

On 25 November 1909, the Carl Rosa Company performed the première in English of Verdi's *La Forza del Destino*. The production was in Manchester. However, Wallace Hartley could not have played on that evening, as we know for a fact that he was hundreds of miles away: Wallace had gone to sea.

Endnotes

1 The original railing, removed like so many others as part of the war effort, has now been replaced.

2 The premises at 28 Ramsden Street are now occupied by a charity shop.

3 At least two more sons were born; Frank Albion in 1900 and Ernest Conrad in 1903 (Conrad was the name of Wallace and Mary's infant brother who died aged one year).

4 The Floral Pavilion is still in existence, but now houses a café and bar.

5 The Beatles, for their album cover *Sergeant Pepper's Lonely Hearts' Club Band*, based their costumes on this kind of uniform, which was typical of the period.

6 Frank Matcham was also responsible for the Opera House in Wakefield, and the Victoria Quarter in Leeds.

7 Renamed the Royal Hall during the First World War in an act of patriotism to avoid the German word 'Kursaal', it still has concerts and provides a venue for conferences.

8 The brassiere (bra) would not be created until 1912, obviating the need for the extremely restricting corsets worn by ladies of fashion.

9 The Firewater Pot was a ceramic vessel specially made for the Savage Club to contain whisky punch. It is now housed, along with Bogg's head dress, in the Leeds Museum's premises at Sovereign Street.

10 Most of the company's archival material is in storage in Liverpool, but, in the absence of a full-time archivist and adequate premises, cannot be consulted at the moment. This situation will change when the company moves into its new headquarters. In the meantime, for details of performances, the company can be contacted at: Carl Rosa Opera, 10 Baltic Place, London, N1 5AQ.

11 In the first edition of this book, based on newspaper articles published at the time of the disaster, I said that Wallace Hartley had joined the Moody-Manners Opera Company later in his career, but now think it more probable that he was with them at an earlier period. With no archives available, it is impossible to be sure.

3

Cunard

A t the end of the nineteenth century, the race for supremacy on the North Atlantic, in terms of size, speed and luxury of the liners, was gathering momentum. The record-breaking Cunarders *Etruria* and *Umbria* had been overtaken by the Inman Co.'s *City of Paris* and *City of New York*, which, in turn, had been overshadowed by the *Majestic* and *Teutonic* of the White Star Line. Not to be outdone, the Cunard Line ordered from the Fairfield Shipbuilding & Engineering Co. another pair of ships, the *Lucania* and the *Campania*, that would put them again in the lead.

It has been suggested that Wallace worked for the White Star Line at some point in his career prior to 1912, but it is practically impossible to check, as the crew lists have been dispersed, and are held in various archives around the world. What we do know is that, in 1909, Wallace joined the Cunard Line. On 16 July, he set sail for New York on board one of the most magnificent ships ever to cross the Atlantic: the *Lusitania*. At a later date, Wallace would also play aboard her sister ship the *Mauretania*.

These two ships were planned in response to the threat posed by the German shipping companies, who were building increasingly larger and faster ships, and had snatched the Blue Riband from England. There was also the fear that Cunard might be swallowed up by a large trust, as had been the fate of the White Star Line, which had been taken over by Morgan's International Mercantile Marine. The British Government, therefore, loaned Cunard the money to build the ships to its own specifications.

The *Lusitania* was built by John Brown & Co. at Clydebank, and the *Mauretania* by Swan Hunter & Whigham Richardson on Tyneside. Both were built to the same dimensions, being 760ft long, with four funnels and quadruple screws. The interiors were designed by different architects, so each ship retained its own individuality. The magnificence of the state rooms and public rooms was unrivalled.

The *Lusitania* was the first of the two leviathans to be launched. She tends to be remembered because her sinking in 1915 by a German torpedo helped to bring America into the First World War.[2] However, she was also a record-breaking pioneer in terms of her size, speed (over 25 knots) and the magnificence of her appointments. The *Lusitania* departed on her maiden voyage from Liverpool to New York on 7 September 1907, to a rapturous crowd of 200,000. The *Mauretania*, which would become the most popular ship on the Atlantic, followed in November of the same year. These beautiful twins became the largest, fastest and most luxurious ships on the Atlantic.

A few months before Wallace Hartley joined the crew of the *Lusitania*, the vessel had been in dry dock in Liverpool, having four-bladed propellers fitted like those of her sister ship, which had proved so successful. However, the *Lusitania* would never be as fast as her sister: she had lost the Blue Riband to the *Mauretania*, who would hold on to it for another twenty years.

On board these ships, Wallace would be playing to some of the richest men and women in the world. He would experience the most luxurious surroundings he had ever encountered. The First Class Dining Saloons were three decks high, crowned with ornate domes, below which there was an elliptical well between the two floors of the dining area. It may have occurred to Wallace Hartley that this arrangement, albeit on a much larger scale, was similar to the one in Collinson's Café.

The First Class Lounge on board the two Cunarders was also called the Music Room as there was a grand piano, situated discreetly to the side, where the orchestra would play. Passengers would gather here to relax and socialise to the strains of the orchestra. Beautifully decorated, these rooms were the epitome of Edwardian grace and elegance.

Wallace Hartley became Second Violin in a band of five musicians on the *Lusitania*. The bandmaster, who had held the post since the ship's maiden voyage, was Charles Cameron, aged thirty-six. Wallace's other fellow musicians were H. Taylor, A. T. Felgate and J. W. Hemingway, whose father had played with Wallace in the municipal

AN INNOVATION
ON THE ENGLISH
LINE.
THE ORCHESTRA PLAYS
DURING ALL MEALS.

Cartoon from the *New York Times* of the band on the *Lusitania*.

band in Bridlington, and remembered him well. The ship's captain was William Turner, who would be in command when she sank.

The orchestra played on the upper floor of the First Class Dining Room at meal times. A humorous cartoon, which appeared in a contemporary edition of the *New York Times*, shows the bandsmen playing on regardless, while the ship lurched and flying objects cascaded around them. A little licence was taken, one feels, by the artist, as a ship of the *Lusitania*'s proportions did not pitch and toss to the degree shown. Interestingly, one of the violinists, with his long, slender limbs and dark, swept-back hair, bears a striking resemblance to Wallace Hartley, and one wonders whether the cartoon was sketched from life.

After dinner, there was dancing in the Dining Room. Tables and chairs were cleared from the centre of the room. Since all the chairs were bolted down, these had to be unscrewed before the dancing could begin, and the dancers had to negotiate their way round the brass plates that were used to anchor the chairs to the deck. The orchestra would play requests for popular tunes of the day. As one purser reported, 'A dance was held in the Saloon Dining Room on the outward voyage, and notwithstanding the brass plates on the deck, the passengers managed to dance round them and spent an enjoyable evening.'

When Wallace Hartley joined Cunard, the bandsmen signed the articles and became members of the crew. There were set rates of pay that had been in operation for some time. For a thirty-day month, the musicians were paid £6 10s. They had to provide their own uniform, but they received a monthly uniform allowance of 10s. In addition, they were allowed to keep a share of any money given on board in the form of gratuities. To put this into perspective, there was a miners' strike in the spring of 1912, which severely affected shipping, as steamships were dependent on coal for power. The miners were demanding 5s per shift.

The Cunard offices at that time were at 8 Water Street, a few doors from the Town Hall and a matter of yards from the Pier Head. The stately Cunard building that now stands between the Liver Building and the Port of Liverpool building was not built until 1917. Wallace may have had to come to the Water Street offices for an initial interview.

In August 1909, shortly after Wallace Hartley joined the company, Cunard liners started to call at Fishguard on the homeward journey, instead of Queenstown, so that passengers for London and the Continent could disembark and the mail could be unloaded.

A round trip across the Atlantic would take approximately twenty days, with five or six days to do each crossing (some trips were slightly faster than others) plus four days in dock in each port. From his parents' home in Dewsbury, it would take him about two hours by train to reach Liverpool, as it was on a direct line from Leeds. When Wallace's ship docked in Liverpool, Maria Robinson would sometimes be there to meet him. From the landing stage, they may have strolled along the Pier Head past the Liver Building, which was under construction; nowadays it is the most famous landmark in the city.

On 14 December 1909, tragedy struck the Robinson household. Maria's father, undoubtedly feeling unwell, went to the premises of Dr Arthur Ellison, who had a practice at Ripley House in Holbeck, near the Robinson mill. While there, Benjamin Robinson died at the age of fifty-one. It is a mark of his respect for and confidence in Maria, that he had singled her out as executor of his will.

Wallace had time to spend with Maria at home, but he also had plenty of time in New York to avail himself of all the city had to offer. The famous tenor Enrico Caruso lived and worked in New York at this period, delighting audiences at the Metropolitan Opera House. Did Wallace go and hear him? It would be nice to think he did. Macy's store had opened in New York, founded by a gentleman called Isidor Straus.

Did Maria ever accompany Wallace on a trip across the Atlantic? The answer to that question is negative, as no one answering to her description appears in the passenger lists for Ellis Island. Was this a missed opportunity or did Wallace prefer to keep his personal and professional lives separate?

In the autumn of 1910, Maria Robinson's younger sister Mary and John Wood were married in Leeds. Wallace was probably at the wedding, as his schedule allowed him time to go home between sailings. Maria was thirty years old and still waiting.

On Saturday 10 September 1910, the *Lusitania* was on her return journey from New York. As was custom, a programme of entertainment was held on board in aid of seamen's charities in Liverpool and New York. The 'Musicale', which took place in the First Class Lounge, opened with the William Tell overture, and featured orchestral pieces as well as vocal performances.

The tradition of the ship's concert went back quite a long way on the Cunard Line. It started as a celebratory evening near the end of the crossing with impromptu and informal entertainment for First Class passengers. In the 1890s, on board the *Lucania* or the *Campania*, no one remembers exactly, the concert took shape from these informal beginnings. It became tradition to appoint an entertainment committee, the most distinguished passenger on board becoming chairman (there were very few chairwomen). As well as featuring the ship's orchestra, the concerts would draw on the uneven talents of the passengers. It also became custom to take up a collection in aid of seamen's charities, the monies being mainly used to help the orphans of seamen in Liverpool. The ship's prettiest ladies were called on to go round amongst the audience during the interval with ribboned baskets. During a concert held on board the *Lusitania* in 1911, £37 11s was collected.

The bandmaster on the *Lusitania* was still Charles Cameron (he appears on the programme as Musical Director), and Wallace was still playing Second Violin. However, the situation was soon to change, as this would turn out to be Wallace's penultimate voyage on the *Lusitania*.

Wallace was offered the post of bandmaster on the *Mauretania*. As such, he would earn the same salary, but any gratuities would be divided into six shares, the bandmaster receiving two shares for himself. The previous bandmaster had been a musician called Morris. Wallace asked Hemingway to transfer with him, but the young man did not accept the invitation.[3] Albert Felgate, who was a pianist, did join Wallace on this new assignment. On 29 October 1910, therefore, Wallace found himself in new company on board the fastest ship on the Atlantic.

Extract from the crew list of RMS *Mauretania*, dated 29 October 1910, showing Wallace Hartley's signature. This was his first voyage as bandmaster on the *Mauretania* and lists his previous ship as the *Lusitania*. (The National Archives, reference BT 100/224)

The *Mauretania*[4] was the favourite ship of many Atlantic travellers, including Franklin D. Roosevelt. She set sail on Saturday 10 December for her Christmas trip, and it turned out to be one of her more memorable voyages. On board were many illustrious passengers, including Prince Albert and Princess Radziwill. The ship left Queenstown at 5.43p.m. and arrived in New York on Friday 16 December. She weighed anchor once again forty-one hours later, and reached Fishguard on Thursday 22 December, thus crossing the Atlantic twice in twelve days, which included the 'turn round' and coaling in New York: an amazing achievement. The following June, the *Mauretania* brought over 2,030 visitors for the Coronation of King George V. To Wallace Hartley, it must have seemed a long, long way from Colne in Lancashire.

In March 1911, with Wallace Hartley as bandmaster, the usual concert was held on board the *Mauretania*, and the total collection for both crossings realised £210 14s 10d, breaking all records.

The cellist in the band, who completed twenty-two round trips with Wallace between 1911 and 1912, was Ellwand Moody.[5] He was from Leeds, and the two men may already have met in music circles in the city. One day, the two men were chatting on board the *Mauretania* and Ellwand Moody, without knowing why, asked Wallace what he would do if he were ever on a sinking ship. Wallace replied, 'I don't think I could do better than play *Oh God Our Help in Ages Past* or *Nearer, My God, to Thee.*'

During one voyage, Wallace recognised an old friend of his father's, Mr Worthington, an Independent Methodist, who preached at Bethel Chapel in Colne, where Albion Hartley had been choirmaster. Wallace, with his affable manner, found time to chat to the older man during the crossing. Mr Worthington recalled this incident on a later occasion.

The *Mauretania* arrived back in Liverpool on 28 November 1911, at the end of one of her routine voyages. On Wednesday 6 December, she was moored on the Mersey, waiting to make the Christmas trip to New York. A strong gale blew up during the evening. By 10.00p.m., the wind was so strong that the mooring cable snapped and she began to drift towards Pluckington Bank. The *Mauretania* was grounded. Within minutes, orders were given to prepare the *Lusitania* for the voyage. The next day, the *Mauretania* was refloated by tugs and taken to Canada Dock, where repairs were carried out. Seven hundred tons of hull plating had to be replaced. The work lasted until the middle of February.

What was Wallace Hartley doing in the meantime? Each of the Cunard liners had its own bandmaster, and the composition of the ship's orchestra changed very little. It may have been difficult for Wallace and his comrades to find temporary positions aboard other Cunard liners, where orchestras already had their full complement. He and the other bandsmen may have been paid a retainer by Cunard, but the situation would change at the beginning of 1912, when musicians would henceforth be supplied to the company by some rather unscrupulous agents from Liverpool. Wallace was no longer an employee of the Cunard Line; technically, he was unemployed.

Wallace was obliged to make alternative temporary arrangements. It was later reported by the *Manchester Evening Chronicle* that, around this time, Wallace had led the orchestra at the Restaurant St James in the city. This restaurant, which had only recently opened, was located at 65 Oxford Street, in the St James Buildings, an imposing edifice that stands on the block between Portland Street and Whitworth Street, next door to the Palace Theatre. Theatre-goers may have dined here before or after performances. The staff of the restaurant would later give a token of their 'respect and esteem' for Wallace Hartley.

This interim would also account for the fact that, in his time with Cunard (at least two years and nine months), Wallace had not made more trips; in that time, he could have made approximately ninety crossings, allowing for time off.

With the *Mauretania* laid up, Wallace found himself at home for Christmas. Wallace was a guest at a young people's party given at the residence of Mrs J. Day, 'a highly respected' Dewsbury lady. Wallace proved to be 'a merry and agreeable companion'. It is not known whether Maria Robinson was with him on that occasion.

At the beginning of 1912, two brothers in Liverpool, C. W. and F.N. Black, put into action a scheme that would have devastating results for sea-going musicians. They had an office on the third floor of No.14 Castle Street, which runs at right angles to Water Street, leading up to the Town Hall. Calling themselves music directors, but nothing more than agents, they proposed to shipping lines that they, the Black brothers, would supply the musicians for the ships' orchestras and give the companies a better deal.

A better deal for the shipping lines meant drastic cuts in wages for the men. They would henceforth receive a mere £4 per month (instead of £6 10s) and no uniform allowance. In addition, the Blacks reserved the right to dismiss any musician without notice at the end of a voyage. The musicians were signed on the articles (i.e. became crew members) at the nominal rate of 1s per month, bringing them within the scope of the Workmen's Compensation Act. The Black brothers already had Cunard and the White Star Line in their pockets, and were probably hoping for a monopoly.

The situation being thus, Wallace Hartley may have decided that, although he loved travelling back and forth across the Atlantic, it may be time to stay ashore and settle down with Maria. The couple planned to marry in the summer.

In March 1912, a delegation from the Amalgamated Musicians' Union approached Bruce Ismay, Managing Director of the White Star Line, asking that the bandsmen be paid directly by the company instead of through an agent, and demanding that they should sign off, as well as sign on, the ship's articles. Ismay was not won over. When the *Olympic* set sail for New York shortly afterwards, the musicians had been booked as Second Class passengers. The musicians' attempt to obtain a fair deal had backfired, but the full implications would not become apparent until a later date.

With the work to her hull completed, the *Mauretania* set sail for New York on 2 March 1912. Because of the new regulations that had been brought in governing ships' musicians, Wallace and the other bandsmen were no longer members of the crew, but travelled as Second Class passengers. Wallace's fellow musicians were: Ernest Drakeford, Frederick Stent, Albert Felgate, pianist, who had been on the *Lusitania* with Wallace, and Ellwand Moody, a cellist from Leeds. Wallace was described as being 5ft 10in tall with a fair complexion, brown hair and blue* eyes. According to the passenger list, their passage had been paid by 'Mr. Black, Liverpool'. All the musicians had to declare that they were neither polygamists nor anarchists! Alongside the musicians' names were the words NON IMMIGRANT ALIEN. And, as such, they arrived in New York.

Wallace Hartley did not know it at the time, but he would only make one more round trip on the *Mauretania*. On Tuesday 19 March, at 7.55a.m., Wallace arrived back in Liverpool. He would have four days before the ship was due to sail again. In the weeks that followed, it was claimed that Wallace had spent some time in Boston Spa with Maria around this time. This was his last opportunity to do so. Little did he realise, when he left her to return to Liverpool, that he would never see her again.

The *Mauretania* left Liverpool on the morning of Saturday 23 March. The following day, she called at Queenstown, before continuing her journey across the Atlantic. Six days later, on Friday 29 March, at 11.25a.m., the *Mauretania* docked in New York. Wallace now had a few days in New York, as the ship was not due to leave until the following Wednesday. Did the men go out and enjoy themselves? We do not know what Wallace did in those last days, but, when the day of departure came round, Wallace embarked on

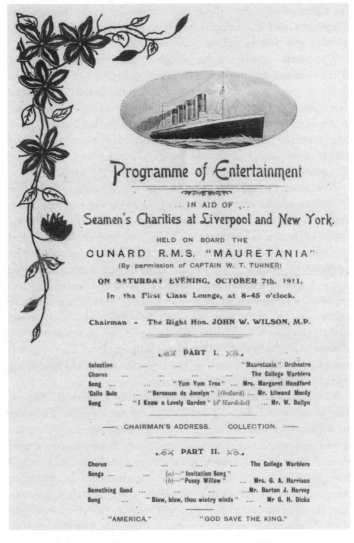

Programme of Entertainment

... IN AID OF ...

Seamen's Charities at Liverpool and New York.

HELD ON BOARD THE

CUNARD R.M.S. "MAURETANIA"

(By permission of CAPTAIN W. T. TURNER)

ON SATURDAY EVENING, OCTOBER 7th, 1911,

In the First Class Lounge, at 8-45 o'clock.

Chairman - The Right Hon. JOHN W. WILSON, M.P.

PART I.

Selection	...	...	...	"Mauretania" Orchestra
Chorus	...	...	...	...	The College Warblers
Song	...	...	"Yum Yum Tree"	...	Mrs. Margaret Handford
'Cello Solo	...	"Berceuse de Jocelyn" (Godard)	...	Mr. Ellwand Moody
Song	...	"I Know a Lovely Garden" (d'Hardelot)	...	Mr. W. Ballyn

—: CHAIRMAN'S ADDRESS.   COLLECTION. :—

PART II.

Chorus	...	...	...	...	The College Warblers
Songs	...	...	(a)—"Invitation Song"		
			(b)—"Pussy Willow"	...	Mrs. G. A. Harrison
Something Good	...	...	...	...Mr. Barton J. Harvey
Song	...	"Blow, blow, thou wintry winds"	...	Mr G. H. Dicks

"AMERICA."   "GOD SAVE THE KING."

A programme of entertainment from on board the *Mauretania*, September 1910. This was the voyage before Wallace joined the crew as bandmaster. His friend, Ellwand Moody, is featured playing a cello solo. (From the collection of the late Jean Elizabeth Martin) his eightieth trip across the Atlantic: it would also be his last. The *Mauretania* left New York at 1.00a.m. on Wednesday 3 April. Wallace Hartley would never set foot on American soil again.

By Sunday evening, the ship was about 200 miles west of Fastnet. The following day, she passed Daunts Rock, near Queenstown, at 4.58a.m., then sailed on to Fishguard, where she arrived at 10.03a.m. Here, passengers had approximately an hour and a half to disembark, as the *Mauretania* departed at 11.34a.m. on the last leg of her journey. She was making good time and arrived in Liverpool, not on Tuesday morning as usual, but on the Monday evening. At 6.00p.m., the *Mauretania* passed Rock Light at the entrance of the Mersey.

On Tuesday 9 April, Wallace left the landing stage in Liverpool to go towards the city centre, probably passing the Liver Building, which now dominated the waterfront. He made his way to the office of the Black brothers on Castle Street, where he was asked to make a momentous decision. The Blacks had a problem. The bandmaster they had hired for the *Titanic*, Percy Ainley of Golcar, had just become a father, and, even in the days before paternity leave, he decided to miss the maiden voyage of the world's largest ship in order to stay at home with his family. The music agents, therefore, had a proposition for Wallace; they wanted him to transfer to the *Titanic*, which was due to set sail the following day. This ship was even bigger than her sister ship the *Olympic*, and would have many wealthy and important people on board.

It was an honour to be asked to be bandmaster on the biggest ship in the world. So why did Wallace hesitate? Firstly, according to Ellwand Moody, he was grieved at being asked to leave the *Mauretania*, where the musicians were 'a very happy and contented family.' There were also practical difficulties. The White Star Line had transferred its New York run to Southampton to get the custom of American tourists who had been on the Continent. It would take him far longer to travel between Yorkshire and Southampton, and the rail fares would be more expensive. Nor would he have time to return home before the *Titanic* sailed. Did the Blacks offer him some pecuniary enticement that their other employees did not enjoy? Suffice it to say that Wallace reluctantly agreed.

Ellwand Moody was also asked to transfer to the *Titanic*, but 'didn't fancy her'. He felt that they were building ships too big and he had a sort of presentiment of disaster; he felt that 'something would happen'. Wallace tried hard to persuade his friend to join him on the

Titanic, but Ellwand Moody told him that he would not accept an engagement on that ship for a preliminary £20.

Moody took leave of Wallace in Liverpool on the Tuesday. He had joined Cunard for a twelve-month contract, which ended on that day. Wallace had not been able to persuade his friend to join him on the *Titanic*, so Ellwand Moody was going back to Leeds. 'Good-bye, old chap,' said Moody, to which Wallace replied, 'I am so sorry you are not going with me.'

The next twenty-four hours would be extremely busy for Wallace Hartley, as the *Titanic* was scheduled to sail the following day, Wednesday 10 April, at 12 noon. There was a railway terminal at the landing stage to take disembarking passengers to London, but Wallace had matters to attend to in the city before leaving, besides which, his journey to Southampton would not take him through London. He would change trains in Reading.

Wallace would not need to go to the White Star Building⁶, as he dealt directly with the Black brothers, but he would need a White Star uniform, complete with White Star buttons and lapel badge. According to the *Manchester Guardian*, this was his first service for the White Star Line. Even if he had already worked for the line, as has been suggested by some, it is unlikely that he had a spare uniform in his luggage. He may have had to go to Messrs J.J. Raynor & Sons to be kitted out.

As was his wont when in Liverpool, Wallace made his way to Brooks's Alley, a narrow street between Church Street and School Lane near the Blue Coat building. Here at No.14 there was a violin-maker called George Byrom. Wallace may have called in for new strings or just for a chat. We know it was a regular call, as, on the Tuesday, a friend of his, Bill, waited for him at the end of the alley and got to Byrom's just after Wallace had left. Instead, he would write to wish him luck.

Wallace also had the more mundane task of sending a parcel of washing home to his mother. He took time to write to his parents to explain to them about his transfer. This he did on headed notepaper from the *Mauretania*. He may have returned to the ship to collect some things, but it is more likely that he wrote the letter on the train, as he would post it at Reading station when he changed trains. He regretted that he would not be able 'to slip over to Dewsbury' to see them this trip, as he usually did, because there would not be time. He concluded with, 'I shall come home the next trip, if it be possible.'

When Wallace Hartley boarded the southbound train in Liverpool, he was embarking on a journey for which there was no return. He was going to be bandmaster on the *Titanic*.

Endnotes

1   The Blue Riband was an honour rather than an award, and was held by the fastest ship to cross the Atlantic.

2   On 7 May 1915, the *Lusitania* was hit by a German torpedo off the coast of Ireland. She sank within eighteen minutes with the loss of 1,198 lives, including many Americans. One torpedo was fired but two explosions were heard, bearing out suspicions that there were munitions aboard.

3   J.W. Hemingway was on board the *Lusitania* when she was torpedoed in 1915. He survived. Charles Cameron, the bandmaster, was not so lucky. His body was recovered off the south coast of Ireland, and was buried in Queenstown in a private grave.

4   When the *Queen Mary* was launched in 1934, the 'Maurie', as she was affectionately known, made her last transatlantic voyage and was subsequently sold for scrap. As she set sail on her final voyage to the breaker's yard in Scotland, with the Blue Peter flying, other ships in Southampton Water sounded their horns as she passed. She paused at the mouth of the Tyne to send a farewell message. Franklin D. Roosevelt said of her, 'If there was ever a ship which possessed the thing called soul, the Mauretania did.' Captain Rostron, commodore of the Cunard Line, who was master of the *Carpathia* in 1912 and later commanded the *Mauretania*, said this of her, 'She had the manners and deportment of a great lady and behaved herself as such.'

5   Moody later claimed that these trips had been on the *Mauretania* but she had been in dock in Liverpool (South Canada and Huskisson) from November 1911 to the end of February 1912.

6   Situated at the corner of James Street and the Strand, the White Star Building stood just behind the buildings on the Pier Head. Designed by the architect of the old Scotland Yard building, it has the same red brick and white stone stripes. The office of Bruce Ismay is said to have been in a turret on the corner of the building.

*   John Wood had previously described Wallace as having dark brown eyes. A subsequent passenger list would describe his eyes as 'grey'. It is likely, therefore, that Wallace's eyes were a deep colour, the shade of which might vary according to the light.

4

Titanic

God Himself could not sink this ship!

I t was a porter answering a lady from First Class, who had asked if the ship was, indeed, unsinkable. Neither the White Star Line nor the builders, Harland & Wolff in Belfast, had ever made such an assertion. For extra safety, the ship had been equipped with bulkheads that ran transversally the whole length of the ship, creating sixteen watertight compartments. This reply displayed the arrogance, rife at the time, that Man and his technology could beat the elements. It was an erroneous assumption that would soon be turned upside down.

The April sunshine was still soft. Excitement was mounting on the White Star dock as more and more people arrived. The first boat train from Waterloo had arrived at 9.30a.m., carrying Second and Third Class passengers. The crew, who had been converging on the dock since sunrise, were now mostly on board, with the exception of a few stragglers. The pier was swarming with people and mountains of luggage. At 10.00a.m., they began to board.

Wallace Hartley and the other bandsmen boarded as Second Class passengers on ticket No.250654. The Second Class entrance was aft on C deck. They would have to find their rooms, no easy task on such a huge vessel. Two rooms, each accommodating five musicians, were set aside for the ship's orchestra. It had probably been envisaged in the grandiose scheme of things, that there would be two ensembles, each comprising five musicians, but, in the last-minute rush, only eight musicians had been engaged. Both rooms were on E deck, but were not adjacent: one of the rooms was next to the potato wash place on port side (no glamour here); the other was on starboard, in Second Class accommodation, near Edwina Troutt, whose cabin number was E101. She would enjoy hearing them practise when she went by.

The musicians were soon back on the upper decks, as the First Class boat train arrived from Waterloo just before 11.30a.m., and there was music to greet them. The First Class entrance was on B deck, where the costliest staterooms were to be found. There were twenty-eight interconnecting rooms to allow the formation of suites, all having rectangular windows, as opposed to portholes, and all in different styles, for example Louis XV, Early Dutch, Regency, French Empire. Here, too, were the two luxury 'millionaire' suites with their private promenade decks, costing £870 for a one-way passage. One of these, on port side, was occupied by Bruce Ismay, President of the White Star Line; the other was empty, as Pierpoint Morgan, head of the trust of which the White Star Line was just a part, had been prevented from sailing.

Before the noon sailing time, the ship was being inspected by passengers and visitors. They must have marvelled at the sumptuous Turkish Baths, the magnificent public rooms, but, above all, the Grand Staircase, 'a gracefully curving staircase, its balustrade supported by light scrollwork of iron with occasional touches of bronze, in the form of flowers and foliage.'[1] At the top was the famous clock, depicting Honour and Glory crowning Time. High above, a great dome of glass and wrought iron threw a flood of light down the stairway. When Wallace Hartley first saw this magnificent dome, his thoughts must have returned to the one in Collinson's Café in Leeds.

On board was the cream of New York and Philadelphia society: Benjamin Guggenheim, Isidor Straus (founder of Macy's store in New York) and his wife, the Wideners and Thayers. Also on board was President Taft's aide-de-camp, Major Archibald Butt, who wrote to his sister, 'If the old ship goes down, you'll find my affairs in ship-shape condition.' The British passengers included the Countess of Rothes, Sir Cosmo Duff-Gordon and his wife Lucy, who, as Lucile, designed expensive gowns and lingerie for rich Edwardian ladies.

The 'spirited' musicians were heard playing American rag-time and a medley from Oskar Strauss' *The Chocolate Soldier*. One passenger who heard them thought that 'their executions of rag-time and operetta were equally delightful.' The eight musicians were divided into a saloon orchestra, comprising five members, and a 'deck band', numbering three. These two ensembles, the quintet and the trio, would play separately throughout the voyage.

As noon approached, people lined the rails of the vessel. Hundreds more had gathered on the pier to see the *Titanic* set sail on her maiden voyage. To a great clamour from passengers and spectators alike, accompanied by the waving of flags and handkerchiefs, the great ship gently left her moorings, and slipped gracefully away towards Southampton Water. To those watching from the quayside she looked 'colossal and queenly'.

However, there was not the same attention for the *Titanic* as there had been for her sister ship, the *Olympic*, which had already been on the Southampton-New York run since June of the previous year. Three ships in total had been planned in response to the Cunarders *Lusitania* and *Mauretania*, which had previously been the largest vessels on the ocean, but, whereas the Cunarders would remain the fastest ships on the Atlantic, the White Star trio would be 'the apotheosis of luxury and comfort' and, in the build-up to the First World War, would demonstrate the 'pre-eminence of the Anglo-Saxon race on the Ocean'. They would also be the largest vessels on the Atlantic. At almost 900ft in length, they were approximately 100ft longer than their Cunard rivals.

The *Titanic* had extra features which were designed as improvements on the *Olympic*. According to Violet Jessop, a stewardess from First Cabin, who had previously served on the *Olympic* since her maiden voyage, the *Titanic* was 'decidedly grander' than the *Olympic* and 'improved in every way'. As well as the luxurious staterooms, the forward half of the Promenade ('A') deck had been glazed to allow more shelter for First Class passengers. This gave the ship her extra tonnage, thereby making her the largest (but only slightly) vessel afloat. It also gave her a distinct exterior from that of her sister ship, the *Olympic*.

Soon it was time for luncheon. The First Class Dining Saloon was on D deck, at the bottom of the Grand Staircase. The largest room afloat and covering the whole width of the ship, the Saloon could accommodate over 500 passengers, the full complement of First Class. It was richly decorated in the Jacobean style, its oak columns painted peanut white. One of the quintet's duties was to play here during luncheon, and there was a grand piano for the purpose. This piano was also used for the regular Sunday service.

The *Titanic* was making her way towards Cherbourg, to pick up passengers who had been in Paris or further afield, mainly Americans, but there were also some steerage passengers from Eastern Europe and Asia Minor. She arrived at dusk. Among the passengers boarding here were Colonel John Jacob Astor, the richest man on board with an estimated fortune of $30 million, and his teenage bride, Madeleine, who were returning from a prolonged honeymoon in Europe and Egypt to allow gossip surrounding their marriage to die down. They had just checked out of the Ritz Hotel in Paris. Also boarding was the Denver socialite Molly Brown, who had happened to meet them in Egypt, and had changed her passage to the *Titanic* when she knew they would also be sailing. She would later be known as the 'Unsinkable'.

When the ship was well under way, the bugle sounded for dinner. The musicians were now playing in the Reception area, where First Class passengers gathered before moving into the Saloon, through the double doors with their delicate wrought-ironwork. Socially, this was the most important time of day on board ship. The women were resplendent in the latest fashions from Paris, set off against the more sombre black of the men's attire. The grand piano was tucked unobtrusively into one of the corners, the orchestra's task being to play discreetly. Although musicians of the highest calibre, they were not 'stars', but merely paid servants. Such orchestras of the time were sometimes required to play from behind palm fronds, heard but not seen; hence the phrase 'Palm Court musicians'.

Music on board ships of the White Star Line was a tradition that went back to the 1850s and possibly beyond, since the formation of the White Star Philharmonic Union & Convivial Society, which arranged entertainment during voyages. The following is an extract from the *White Star Journal* of 12 May 1855:

> The more serious business of the day, however, begins at 7 o'clock in the evening. The band, which through the day have played listlessly and at intervals, now nerve themselves for serious work … a brisk succession of polka, waltz, quadrille and country dance is kept up with great vigour…

A First Class passenger travelling from Southampton to Queenstown remarked, 'After dinner, we sat in the beautiful lounge listening to the White Star orchestra playing *The Tales of Hoffman* and *Cavalleria Rusticana* selections.'

However, there must be some mistake here, as the quintet played in the Reception area outside the Dining Saloon after dinner. The time in question was probably late afternoon when tea was served in the lounge, as the quintet played here every afternoon as part of their routine. Situated on A (or Promenade) deck, the lounge was the epitome of Edwardian elegance, decorated in the style of Louis XV, its walls covered in fine boiseries.[3]

By lunchtime on the following day, the *Titanic* had reached Queenstown (now called Cobh, pronounced 'Cove'), situated in Cork Harbour. Here the Irish emigrants embarked, to find their accommodation in Third Class quite comfortable, conditions being quite unlike those on board the early ships that had taken people to a new life across the ocean. This was *Titanic's* last stop. She now sailed off gloriously into the open Atlantic. At dusk, Ireland was fading into the distance. The *Titanic* would never see dry land again.

Wallace Hartley posted a letter home from Queenstown. Written on headed notepaper, 'On board RMS *Titanic*',[4] it joined the sacks of mail that had been loaded on to the tender *America*:

> Just a line to say we have got away all right. It has been a bit of a rush but I am just getting a little settled. This is a fine ship and there ought to be plenty of money around. We have a fine band and the boys seem very nice. I've missed coming home very much and it would have been nice to have seen you all, if only for an hour or two, but I could not manage it. (The ship would get back to Southampton a fortnight on Saturday). Shall probably arrive home on the Sunday morning. All love, Wallace.

Wallace Hartley was not the only one to refer to male colleagues on board ship as 'boys', regardless of their age. The reason the boys in the band[5] merely *seemed* very nice was because Wallace had not met any of them before, and was just getting to know them. There were two other violinists beside himself: John Law ('Jock') Hume, a twenty-one-year-old from Dumfries and a Belgian, Georges Krins, twenty-three, whose address was in London. Jock played Second Violin in the quintet and Krins, who had studied for six years at the Conservatoire in Liège, was in the trio. According to Violet Jessop, the young stewardess, Jock, was 'always so eager and full of life'. This was his first position on board a ship.

There were two pianists on board: Percy Taylor, of Clapham, and Theodore Brailey, an only son, who also lived in London. It was probably Brailey who played in the trio, as he was the younger of the two men. Brailey had just transferred from the *Carpathia*. Indeed, a waiter on the *Carpathia*, Robert Vaughan, seventeen, had been

The White Star Orchestra. From left to right: Wallace Hartley standing, Percy Taylor on the piano, Jock Hume, Second Violin, Fred Clarke on double bass and John Woodward, cellist. This was the quintet and performed separately from the trio. (Drawing by Jean Elizabeth Martin)

talking to two musicians who were to transfer to the *Titanic*. 'At least we'll get some decent grub,' one had remarked.

The two cellists were John Wesley Woodward, from Oxfordshire, and a Frenchman, Roger Bricoux, who was from Lille. Bricoux, twenty-one, was a native of Monte Carlo, where his father was a member of the Casino Orchestra. Roger himself had played at the Grand Central Hotel in Leeds for twelve months, and his joviality had won him many friends in the city. He was the other musician who had transferred from the *Carpathia:* he and Brailey had left the ship in New York on 2 April.

The eighth musician was Frederick Clarke, twenty-eight, a bass player from Liverpool, who was also making his first trip across the

Wallace Hartley in his White Star uniform, which was navy blue with green lapels. (Drawing by Jean Elizabeth Martin)

Atlantic. For a time, he had played at the Kardomah Café on Church Street, one of the main thoroughfares in Liverpool.

The fact that the *Titanic* had eight musicians was another added feature; the *Olympic* only had five. The trio was quite separate from the others, and had different duties. Whereas the quintet played the routine ship's business, such as concerts, meal-times and Sunday service, the trio's main task was to play for the First Class passengers in the reception area outside the *A la Carte* Restaurant at the foot of the main stairway aft. Here there was ample accommodation for musicians, partly recessed and raised on a platform. This restaurant was another feature peculiar to the *Titanic* and was frequented by the ship's elite. Situated on B deck aft, it was decorated in the style of Louis XIV, with wall panelling and chairs in French walnut, silk curtains and a rich Axminster carpet. Here the cuisine was as good as any hotel on shore.

To the side of the *A la Carte* Restaurant, with access both from the restaurant itself and the Reception area where the trio played, was the *Café Parisien*, situated on a covered promenade, emulating a continental pavement café, with its French waiters and casual wicker furniture. The café proved very popular; one survivor remarked that it was like an exclusive club for the rich and famous on board, who would adjourn here after meals for coffee and social chit-chat.

The trio itself had a continental flavour with the French cellist, Roger Bricoux, and the Belgian violinist, Georges Krins. The pianist was probably Theo Brailey, as he had previously worked with Bricoux, and he was the younger of the two pianists on board. Among those who enjoyed the atmosphere in the *Café Parisien* were Colonel Archibald Gracie, and the others in his 'coterie'. Gracie told his spectacular survival story in a book published not long after the disaster. Together they would listen to the 'always delightful music of the Titanic's band'.

The Edwardians enjoyed a wide range of music from opera to music-hall. There were no barriers; music was not considered 'high-brow' or 'low-brow'. The musicians played from the White Star Line Music Book, which contained 352 pieces of music, ranging from operetta, ouvertures, waltzes, marches, cakewalks and even sacred music. No foxtrot music was included, although the dance had been invented. Indeed, there were no organised 'dances' as such on board White Star liners, but this did not preclude spontaneous dancing. In addition, the musicians had to know popular tunes of the day, and be able to respond to requests from passengers. Wallace Hartley had taken the current popular pieces *The Bunny Hop* and *The Turkey Trot* on board. No sheet music was allowed: the musicians had to be able to play a piece on hearing its number when called by the bandleader, hence the origin of pieces of music being referred to as 'numbers', (e.g. 'a catchy little number'). Wallace himself was the composer of a few 'clever numbers', which he doubtlessly had on board with him.

The band was immensely popular with passengers, Wallace Hartley and his men being always obliging with regard to requests. Wallace himself is said to have had a 'showman's smile'. However, there are always some customers who are not easy to please. Violet Jessop, in her role as stewardess, had to deal with several passengers in First Class who proved very difficult. One lady had been blacklisted by another shipping line because of her 'unreasonable behaviour' and 'demoralising effect on passengers'. There were on board, therefore, a few critics of the band, notably in Archibald Gracie's clique, who felt it was poor on Wagner. Remembering that the musicians were limited to the repertoire and there were only two pieces of

Wagner in the White Star Line Music Book, did these passengers
really think that Wagner's music was suited to an ensemble
comprising only five musicians, with no brass or percussion? There
were others, probably not very musical themselves, who said the
'violin was weak'. Perhaps these criticisms reflect more badly on the
critics than the musicians.

While on board, Wallace made the acquaintance of a couple from
Second Class, Mr John James Ware and his wife Florence Louise
(Florrie), both in their early thirties, who were making their way
to Connecticut, where John was going to set himself up in the
carpentry business. Why they became friendly is not known; perhaps
their cabins in Second Class were in close proximity.

The days slipped by with the same routine on board. Sunday was
not so sunny as the other days. As always on board ship, divine service
was held at 10.30a.m. in the First Class Dining Saloon. The service,
conducted by the Captain, was not from the Church of England
Book of Common Prayer, but from the White Star Line's own prayer
book, and included the 'Prayer for Those at Sea'. The music for the
hymns was provided by the musicians from the quintet, as part of
their routine duties. The service concluded shortly after 11.00a.m.
with the hymn *Oh God Our Help in Ages Past*. One of the hymns was
Eternal Father, Strong to Save, which ends with the line: 'For those in
peril on the sea.'

Mr Charles Hays, President of the Canadian Grand Trunk
Railroad, who was a passenger in First Class, prophesied:

> The White Star, the Cunard and the Hamburg-Amerika lines are now
> devoting their attention to a struggle for supremacy in obtaining the
> most luxurious appointments for their ships, but the time will come
> soon when the greatest and most appalling of all disasters at sea will
> be the result.

His prophesy would soon come true and he himself would lose his
life.

Dinner-time on the last evening came round. The First Class
menu included oysters, filet mignon Lili, Waldorf pudding and
French ice cream, after which, in the words of sisters Mrs Martha
Eustis Stephenson and Miss Elizabeth Eustis, there was 'a fine
musical programme in the Reception Room', the music provided,
of course, by the quintet. Alfred Fernand Omont from Le Havre,

who was one of the passengers boarding at Cherbourg, remembered: 'After dinner there was the orchestra playing in the companion-way and the Captain was there.'

According to Violet Jessop, Jock Hume, whom the stewardess took to be the bandmaster, told her in his rich Scotch accent that he was going to give them 'a real tune, a Scotch tune to finish up with.' Although he was in a position to do no such thing, to Violet the music on that last evening was 'at its gayest'. Chief Steward Edward Wheelton, remembering the last evening, said: 'There had been dancing and music on board.'

During the course of the concert, the musicians played some Puccini for Mrs Churchill Candee, a writer, who was in Archibald Gracie's 'coterie'. They probably played a selection from *Madame Butterfly* from the White Star Line Music Book. They also played some Dvorak for Hugh Woolner, the piece in question in all likelihood being the *Humoresque*, which was also in the White Star Line Music Book. By 11.00p.m. passengers started to retire and the concert ended with *Tales of Hoffman*, remembered some time later with a shudder by the Countess of Rothes.

Later that night, Miss Elizabeth W. Shutes would be back on deck in completely different circumstances: 'We passed by the palm room, where, two short hours before, we had listened to a beautiful concert … And the music went on, and the ship went on.'[6]

Endnotes

1   Extract from a White Star publication, used as publicity for the ship.
2   The third ship, the *Britannic*, would enter service as a hospital ship during the First World War. She, too, was sunk, but it was a German mine in the Aegean that was to blame. She has since been discovered in relatively shallow waters, and there are plans afoot to convert her into the first underwater museum in the world, enabling the lucky ones to view a ship that was structurally, if not in appointments, identical to the *Titanic*.
3   Although Edward VII had been succeeded by his son, George V, the fashions, tastes and spirit of the Edwardian era remained.
4   The *Titanic* was a Royal Mail Ship, hence the initials.
5   The addresses of the bandsmen are as follows:
    Wallace Henry Hartley, Surreyside, West Park Street, Dewsbury, Yorkshire.
    John Law Hume, 42 George Street, Dumfries, Scotland.
    Percy Cornelius Taylor, 9 Fentiman Road, Clapham, London.
    John Wesley Woodward, The Firs, Windmill Road, Headington, Oxon. Aged thirty-two years, he had joined the White Star Line in 1909, and was on

board the *Olympic* when she collided with the *Hawke*, narrowly escaping injury.

Roger Marie Bricoux, 5 Place du Lion d'Or, Lille, France.

John Frederick Preston Clarke, 22 Tunstall Street, Smithdown Road, Liverpool. Unmarried, he lived with his mother and sisters in the city. He had left Liverpool from Woodside station the Sunday before the *Titanic* sailed.

Georges Alexandre Krins, 10 Villa Road, Brixton, London.

W. Theodore Brailey, 71 Lancaster Road, Ladbroke Grove, London.

6 From her manuscript 'When the *Titanic* went down', Miss Shutes must have meant the *Café Parisien*. The Palm Court or Verandah was situated just above on A deck, with doors leading out from the First Class Smoking Room. In actual fact, it was two rooms, one on either side of the ship.

5

A Brilliantly Beautiful Starlit Night

The sea was like a millpond. There was no moon that night and not a single cloud. All around, stars descended right down to the horizon. To Lawrence Beesley, who had been strolling on deck, it was 'a brilliantly beautiful starlit night'.

Two seamen were on duty in the crow's nest. They had been told to look out for icebergs, as the ship was approaching the Labrador current, south of Cape Race. In spring, when temperatures rise, huge chunks of glaciers on the western coast of Greenland break off and float away as icebergs, in a process known as calving. Temperatures had been falling all evening, and it was now penetratingly cold, a sign that icebergs were near. Passengers taking a last walk on deck shivered and went back indoors.

Titanic was racing ahead at 22.5 knots, in spite of ice warnings from various ships. She was approaching the Grand Banks off Newfoundland, and had reached latitude 41° 46' North and longitude 50° 14' West. Suddenly, Frederick Fleet in the crow's nest spotted a huge, black mass looming up directly in front of them. He rang the bell three times, the signal for danger, and phoned down to the bridge, 'Iceberg straight ahead!' First Officer Murdoch gave the order, 'Hard a-starboard!' to turn the ship to port, and ordered the engines to be put into reverse to slow the ship down. At first, nothing seemed to happen, and there were several seconds of the utmost suspense as the ship headed straight for the iceberg, but, finally, the ship veered to port, and they sailed past the iceberg, which towered about 80ft above the water level. It was now 11.40p.m.

A few First Class passengers were still playing cards in the Smoking Room on 'A' deck. Some rushed out and saw chunks of ice breaking off and tumbling onto the decks or into the sea. Some Third Class passengers started to kick the ice round the well-deck in an impromptu game of football. Molly Brown, dressed from head to foot in black velvet, was walking on the Promenade deck with a friend. They were aware of a bump, and sauntered round the deck to see what had happened. Most of the passengers were in bed, unaware that anything had occurred. To Frederick Fleet in the crow's nest it seemed like 'a close shave'. In the First Class staterooms, some had noticed 'a faint, grinding jar', or 'a rumbling, scraping noise', others a vague shudder. But in steerage on the starboard side, they heard 'a tremendous noise' as the ice below the water level scraped past the ship. In the boiler rooms, there was an ear-splitting crash, and the sea cascaded in. First Officer Murdoch rang the warning signal and pressed the button to close the watertight emergency doors in the boiler rooms. The engines were now stopped.

By 11.50p.m., water began to flow into the lowest steerage accommodation at the bow and into the mail room. Captain Smith was now on the bridge, and had sent for Thomas Andrews, Managing Director of Harland & Wolff, who made a tour of the ship with the carpenter to assess the damage. Bruce Ismay, who had been awakened by the jolt, rushed onto the bridge in his slippers to find out what was wrong.

The *Titanic* had struck the iceberg with the force of over a million foot-tons. Thomas Andrews made some calculations. The ship's plates, which were less than an inch thick, had buckled inwards at intervals for a length of 300ft, flooding five compartments. The watertight compartments only went up as far as E deck. As the first ones flooded, the water would gradually spill over into the others. It was now mathematically impossible for the *Titanic* to stay afloat. (She could have survived if only four compartments had flooded, or, ironically, if the ship had hit the iceberg head on.) The vessel that was widely considered to be unsinkable was about to founder.

At 12.05a.m., therefore, Captain Smith ordered Chief Officer Wilde to uncover the lifeboats, and First Officer Murdoch to muster the passengers, knowing that there were only enough places in the boats for about half the people on board. He then went to the wireless room, where First Operator Jack Phillips, and his assistant, Harold Bride, had been busy sending frivolous messages on behalf of

First Class passengers. An hour earlier, the Leyland liner *Californian* had tried to contact the *Titanic*, but Phillips was so busy he told the ship's radio operator to 'shut up'. Tragically, a warning from the Atlantic Transport Line ship *Mesaba*, informing them that the ice field lay straight ahead, did not reach the bridge.

At first, it was as though nothing had happened, but, gradually, people started to realise that the ship had stopped, although there was as yet no outward sign of danger. Some First Class passengers were gathering in the magnificent foyer on the Promenade deck, at the top of the first flight of the Grand Staircase, above the ornate clock. Colonel Archibald Gracie, aroused by a 'sudden shock' and one of the first up, was among them, and noticed a list on the companionway. As more passengers were summoned from their staterooms by the stewards, there was more activity, with people wandering about, wondering what to do next and struggling to get into their lifejackets.

It was now 12.15a.m., and the band started to play in the First Class Lounge, while passengers milled around. They were wearing their regular dark blue tuxedo-style uniforms with green facings and White Star lapel badges. The musicians had gathered in a haphazard way, as they were accommodated in separate rooms, separated by bulkheads. Pierre Maréchal, a survivor from First Class, declared that the musicians had received an order to play all the time without stopping, so as to avoid a panic.[1] One report says that it was Purser McElroy, acting on the captain's orders, who gave these instructions. This is probably the case, as the two men were seen together shortly afterwards. Kate Buss saw a group of musicians carrying their instruments in the Second Class section of 'E' deck. She knew that something was wrong. According to one report, the musicians had been 'chaffed by passengers, who thought they were running to rescue their instruments.'

Violet Jessop, the stewardess, on her way up to the boat deck, ran into the band as they made their way towards the lounge. 'Funny, they must be going to play,' she thought, 'and at this late hour!' Jock Hume smiled in passing; she thought he looked rather pale. 'Just going to give them a tune to cheer things up a bit.' Nearby, on the companionway, stood Captain Smith with Purser McElroy and Bruce Ismay. Presently the strains of the band reached Violet as she stood on the boat deck.

The eight bandsmen, a quintet and a trio, had probably never played together before. Only seven musicians could play, as there was only one piano in the lounge. Jack Thayer remembers them playing to a restless crowd going to and fro through the lounge and not paying much attention. Major Peuchen, gambler George Brereton and May Futrelle, wife of American writer Jacques, all recognised Irving Berlin's *Alexander's Rag-time Band*, a great hit of the time.[2] Published in 1911, it had made him America's top song-writer by the end of the year, and, by the end of 1912, over two million copies of the song had been sold in the United States alone. Mrs Futrelle remembered that, while this piece was being played, she saw stokers rush past 'with the fear of death in their faces'.

On the boat deck, the lifeboats were being cleared. There were sixteen all together, plus four collapsible Engelhardt boats. All boats together could carry 1,178 people: there were 2,207 on board. None of the passengers and few of the crew knew this. At this stage, people were not worried and remained calm, but did not know what to do as there had been no boat drill and they had no boat assignments. The crew had assignments, but hardly any had bothered to look. At 12.20a.m., the lifeboats had been swung out ready for loading, but there were few people on deck at this time.

The boats were all numbered: even numbers on port side, odd on starboard, starting from the bow. Second Officer Charles Lightoller was in charge of the boats on port side, while First Officer Murdoch was on starboard. Lightoller got the word from Captain Smith, 'Put the women and children in the boats and lower away.' He began with boat No.6, which was positioned just across from the First Class entrance, where the band was now playing.

The musicians had moved up to the foyer on the boat deck when the passengers were being mustered. One of the pianists may still have been able to play at this point, as it is believed that there was an upright piano (some say an Aeolian organ, although neither is apparent in photographs) on the landing at the top of the Grand Staircase. The First Class passengers had sauntered out of the lounge, past the band in the foyer and out on to the boat deck. Then, when the lifeboats were being loaded, the interior of the ship became quite deserted.

Before moving outside, the musicians may have had to collect their overcoats and lifejackets from E deck. Jock Hume and Fred Clark wrapped mufflers round their necks against the cold night air. They then took up positions just outside the port-forward First Class entrance, opposite boat No.6, where they remained. The cellists must have equipped themselves with seats, as they could not play in a standing position. It is not known what the pianists, Percy Taylor and Theodore Brailey, were doing, but one can only assume that they were on hand, giving their support to the other bandsmen. Second Officer Lightoller later wrote in his autobiography, 'Passing along to No.6 boat to load and lower, I could hear the band playing cheery sort of music. I don't like jazz music as a rule, but I was glad to hear it that night. I think it helped us all.' What Lightoller heard was not, in fact, jazz, which was not invented until after the First World War, but rag-time.

At 12.25a.m., the Cunarder *Carpathia*, which was outbound from New York, sent the message, 'Coming hard', but she was fifty-eight miles away, and it would take her four hours to reach the stricken ship. The *Titanic*'s sister ship, the *Olympic*, which had set sail from New York on the Saturday, had also picked up the C.Q.D. distress signal and was on her way, but she was even further away at 500 miles.

Lawrence Beesley, a Second Class passenger, was on deck at 12.40a.m.: 'I saw a bandsman come round the vestibule corner from the staircase entrance, Second Class, and run down the now deserted starboard deck, his cello trailing after him, the spike dragging along the floor.' One survivor, Bertha Lehmann, remembered being helped into her lifejacket and escorted to a lifeboat by a French-speaking musician, but he made no attempt to get into the boat. This must have been Roger Bricoux, who was hurrying to join the other bandsmen.

Archibald Gracie considered the band's playing 'a wise provision, tending to allay excitement.' He did not recognise any of the tunes, but remembers that they were all cheerful. Edwina Troutt, standing forward on the port side, not far from the band, remembered hearing Elgar's *Land of Hope and Glory*. Some survivors recall a pretty, English melody called *In the Shadows*, which was very popular in 1911. Others claimed they heard *The Star Spangled Banner*.

At 12.45a.m., the first boat, No.7, was lowered. There were only nineteen or twenty people on board. Women were reluctant to leave their husbands, as they could see no danger, and felt safer on the ship than in a little boat on the ocean. The going was so slow that First Officer Murdoch felt he could not wait any longer.

It was at the same time that the first rocket was fired to alert any vessels in the vicinity. A light flickered tantalizingly on the horizon; it was later known that this was the *Californian*, who had sent the

A music book given out to passengers so that they could request tunes to be played by the orchestra. In this one are 341 pieces that the band had to know off by heart.

iceberg warning, and herself had shut down her engines, and her radio, for the night. The brilliant light from the rocket lit up the startled faces on deck. This desperate plea for help made people realise how serious the situation really was. They were now more willing to get into the boats.

Daniel Marvin, a nineteen year old from New York's fashionable society, and his eighteen-year-old bride, were returning from honeymoon. 'It's all right, little girl,' he said. 'You go. I'll stay a while.' He blew her a kiss as she got into the boat. He did not attempt to get into any other boat. Mrs Isidor Straus, wife of the founder of Macy's store in New York, flatly refused to leave her husband, and would not get into a boat. When the rockets started to go up, Emily Ryerson heard her husband saying, 'Don't you hear the band playing?' Their music gave a tone of normality to the whole proceedings, giving the impression that there was nothing wrong, thereby maintaining calm.

The deck was now slanting more. Thomas Andrews knew that time was of the essence, and walked from boat to boat, urging the ladies to get in. Molly Brown, in her rather loud way, was also urging ladies to get into the boats. When Second Officer Lightoller at boat No.6 asked if there were any more ladies, two gentleman friends of Molly's said, 'Here's a lady!' and threw her into the boat. At 12.55a.m., boat No.6 was launched. Molly Brown later told reporters: 'After we reached the water, we watched the ship. We could hear the band. Every light was showing.'

At 1.00a.m., boat No.3 was launched, and at 1.10a.m. boat No.8 followed. Boat No.1, with a capacity for forty passengers, was lowered with twelve people aboard, only two of whom were ladies. During the loading of the lifeboats, a dramatic moment occurred when a woman fell between one of the boats and the ship, but was somehow caught by passengers on the deck below, and hauled to safety.

Meanwhile, in the engine room, the men remained at their posts in order to keep the steam up, the lights on and the pumps going. From the boats, the passengers could see the lights blazing in all the portholes, but now they were on a hopeless slant. They could also hear the band; they were still playing cheerful music. Playing in those temperatures must have been difficult. Although they were wearing overcoats, the musicians' fingers must have become quite cold and they may have had to re-tune their instruments because of the effects of the temperature on the strings. Marshall Drew, who was eight at the time, said, 'Waiting on the deck … I could hear the ship's orchestra playing somewhere off towards First Class.'

Shortly before 1.30a.m., Mr John Ware and his wife Florence, running towards the boats on portside, passed the band. Florence, wearing only a nightgown in her haste, must have looked cold. Wallace handed her his silver hip flask, the contents of which would help to ward off the cold on the icy sea.[3] She boarded boat No.12 and rowed most of the night. Did Wallace think that the empty flask would be returned once they reached dry land?

By 12.55a.m., five rockets had been fired to no avail. Captain Smith asked the quartermaster to use a Morse code lamp to alert the ship on the horizon. This too had no effect.

Orders had been issued at 12.30a.m. to send women and children from steerage up to the boat deck. Many Third Class passengers gathered on E deck at the foot of the main steerage staircase. More kept arriving, dragging luggage along the long corridor that went the length of the ship, known to the crew as 'Scotland Road'. They were noisy and confused; many did not understand the directions they were given, as they did not speak English. Many simply could not find their way through the labyrinth of corridors and stairways. On some staircases leading to Second or First Class, the barriers, installed as requirements by US immigration, had not been opened. One steward led a couple of parties up to the boat deck, and some managed to climb up cranes from the well-deck, but, in the confusion, the vast majority were left milling around below until it was too late.

By 1.45a.m., water had flooded the forward well-deck. Those remaining on board were now quite eager to leave the ship. A crowd of men raced forward to boat No.14. Fifth Officer Lowe fired down the side of the ship as a warning. As collapsible C was ready to be lowered, Bruce Ismay, President of the White Star Line, who was still in his slippers after rushing to and fro all evening, suddenly got in. He would remain a social outcast for the rest of his life.

The water was now up to C deck, but the music could still be heard. All the portholes were still ablaze, but the passengers in the lifeboats noticed that the lights were slipping underwater one by one, suffusing the water with a green, eerie glow. Only two boats were left. John Jacob Astor's young, pregnant wife, Madeleine, was helped into boat No.4 by her husband. He stayed behind. Daniel Buckley from Third Class jumped into the boat and hid under Mrs Astor's shawl.

At 2.05a.m., with many passengers still on board, the last boat, collapsible D, was lowered. When all the boats had gone, some of the men started jumping overboard. Among them was George Broden of Los Angeles, who later declared that, when he jumped, the band was still playing.

Benjamin Guggenheim, the second richest man on board, refused to put on a lifejacket and declared: 'We are dressed in our best and are prepared to go down like gentlemen.'

Captain Smith paid a last visit to the wireless room, where Phillips was still feverishly trying to make contact, now using the new SOS signal. He said, 'I release you.' But Phillips kept on working. Outside, the bandsmen were now wearing lifejackets over their coats, and were still playing lively tunes to maintain morale. Mrs Gold, who left in one of the last lifeboats, was 'specially struck by a glimpse of a violinist playing steadily with a great lifebelt in front of him.'

At 2.10a.m., a steward walked into the First Class Smoking Room to find Thomas Andrews all alone. His lifebelt was thrown over the green baize of a card table. The steward asked him, 'Aren't you going to have a try for it, Mr Andrews?' He never answered or moved, but 'just stood like one stunned', staring aft towards the magnificent mantelpiece.[4]

Lightoller, Murdoch and others were frantically trying to launch collapsibles A and B, which were stored on top of the officers' quarters. It was proving an extremely difficult task. Collapsible A was launched, but the sides were left down, while the other fell onto the deck and remained upside down.

At this point, with water rising treacherously fast, the band struck up their last piece of music. Legend has it that the band played the hymn *Nearer, My God, to Thee*. In fact, everyone seemed to hear something different, or nothing at all. Harold Bride ran out of the wireless room towards collapsible B: 'From aft came the tunes of the band. There was a rag-time tune, I don't know what, and then there was Autumn.' Colonel Archibald Gracie declared that no hymns were played; he thought that this would have been a tactless reminder to people of imminent death and more likely to cause a panic. Greaser Thomas Ranger, having come up on deck after turning off forty-five fans to find that all the boats had gone, heard the band still playing.

A Mrs A.A. Dick from Calgary originated the legend of what was played last by stating emphatically, 'What we remember best was that, as the ship sank, we could hear the band playing *Nearer, My God, to Thee*. We looked back and could see the men standing on deck, absolutely quiet and waiting for the end.' The story seemed to be embroidered every time it was repeated, and, in some reports, the musicians played with water up to their knees, although this would have been physically impossible.

Whatever was played, the music floated over the calm water and could be heard by the people in the boats. Women listened in wonder. Molly Brown joined in with her enormous trained voice, although she did not know the words, but noticed that the ship was now at an angle of 45 degrees. There was an 'agonising stateliness about the moment.' On the ship, the people left behind were not paying much attention to the music, as everyone started to move towards the poop deck.

When the band stopped playing, this seemed to be the signal for the end. The bow was now submerged. Water came over the steel half-wall, pouring onto the bridge and the boat deck, a few feet from where the band were standing. At this moment a crowd of steerage passengers, men, women and children, surged up from below decks. There was frantic movement now as people rushed aft.

Although he and the other bandsmen had stayed at their post until all the boats had gone and there was no hope of escape, Wallace Hartley did not plan on dying that night. At some point in the next ten minutes or so, Wallace took care to strap his violin case to his chest in order to leave his arms free for holding on, and later for swimming.

When the bow went under, a big wave swept up the deck and washed collapsible B off the ship. Lightoller dived into the water, which was now lapping round his feet, and swam off, while wireless operator Harold Bride found himself under the upturned boat. When he emerged, 'There were men all around me, hundreds of them. The sea was simply dotted with them … She [the ship] was a beautiful sight then. Smoke and sparks were rushing out of her funnel.' Colonel Archibald Gracie was sucked down, but, being a strong swimmer, he was eventually able to resurface. Chef John Collins was holding a baby belonging to a Third Class woman. He was swept overboard by the wave, the water washing the baby out of his grasp.

The stern was rising higher and higher. Deckchairs and people started to slide down the decks, and others could be seen from the boats clinging to winches, anything they get could hold of, like swarms of bees. An enormous crashing noise could be heard, possibly the breaking up of the ship, as the angle of the stern increased. The forward funnel broke loose and smashed down, crushing some of the swimmers.

To get a better idea of what happened to the band and the others who were left on the ship at this time, we have the testimony of

Mrs Rosa Abbott, a Third Class passenger and the only woman to be rescued from the sea that night. As the stern rose higher, people were thrown overboard, falling on top of one another and colliding with objects. Many were injured in the fall. Mrs Abbott had been on the well-deck with her two sons of nine and fifteen. She held them close, but lost her grip as they went over and they were lost. She was struck by falling people from different angles and by wreckage rising to the surface. Several of her ribs were broken and she was badly battered and bruised. She eventually climbed onto collapsible A, which was completely swamped with water, and had to remain standing until being picked up by Officer Lowe. Most of those who fell or jumped overboard hit the water between 2.10a.m. and 2.15a.m., several minutes before the ship sank completely.

Chief baker Charles Joughin, fortified with whisky, climbed onto the outside of the starboard rail when the deck became too steep to stand on, and climbed round to the stern, waiting for the vessel to plunge. The ship was now perpendicular. He glanced at his watch: it was 2.15.a.m.

The *Titanic* stood out black and massive against the starlit sky. She bobbed for a while like a cork, with all her lights out, and then started to dive, with ever-increasing momentum. To baker Joughin it was like being on an elevator. The people in the boats gazed awestruck at this final scene. The ship slipped from view. It was 2.20a.m.

Fifteen hundred people were now thrashing about helplessly and hopelessly. The water was below freezing. Charles Lightoller said, 'Striking the water was like a thousand knives being driven into one's body.' Colonel Archibald Gracie said that when he resurfaced, 'There arose to the sky the most horrible sounds ever heard by mortal man, except by those of us who survived this terrible tragedy.' Lawrence Beesley, who was in one of the boats, later wrote, 'The cries of many hundreds of our fellow passengers, struggling in the ice-cold water … filled us with stupefaction.'

Lightoller, Gracie, Harold Bride, Jack Phillips, Charles Joughin, about thirty in all, found themselves on upturned collapsible B, and spent the night upright, trying desperately not to capsize the boat.

The lifeboats had not been filled to capacity. Molly Brown, who had 'a heart as big as a ham', draped her sable stole round a stoker, who was wearing nothing over his singlet, and probably saved his life. She and several other passengers in different boats suggested that they turn back and pick up some of those struggling in the water, but they were all over-ruled. Only one boat did turn back, under the orders of Fifth Officer Lowe and, altogether that night, only thirteen of those 1,500 were eventually picked up. Wallace Hartley was not one of them.

The cries of the people in the water lasted about an hour. At first they shivered uncontrollably, then their limbs gradually went numb. They floated quietly in the darkness, buoyed up by their lifebelts. Their cries grew weaker as, gradually, one by one, they lost consciousness. The noise died down to individual cries in the night.

August Wennerstrom was standing in collapsible A. A friend, who was in the water, was clinging to the boat. After about half an hour Wennerstrom turned to his friend, who seemed to have aged sixty years: 'His face had sunk in, his hair and moustache were grey, his eyes had changed ... He just looked straight ahead, never made a move or said a word.' He had frozen to death. Very few drowned that night. The 1,500 people in the water, including all the bandsmen, died from the intense cold in the icy waters of the North Atlantic.

Endnotes

1   Pierre Maréchal was talking to Secretary Williams of the Amalgamated Musicians' Union, who made a written report.

2   Irving Berlin was hailed in London as the King of Rag-time. In Europe, the song was credited with starting the craze for American syncopation, but there was very little syncopation in the music, in spite of the title. Berlin was later to say, 'You know, I never did find out what rag-time was', and, on another occasion, 'No-one was more flabbergasted than I was at the smashing hit it made.'

3   The silver flask with its close-fitting cup stood 133mm high and was made by James Dixon & Son of Sheffield in 1900. It bore the monogram W.H.H. and was later inscribed with the words, 'Given to Aunt Florence by the Bandmaster of RMS *Titanic*, April 15, 1912'. In her interview for the *Bristol Times and Mirror* on 11 May, she made no reference to the above incident.

4   An exclusively male preserve, the First Class Smoking Room was panelled with mahogany, inlaid with mother-of-pearl. Above the fireplace was a painting, 'Plymouth Harbour', by Norman Wilkinson. A sister painting, 'Approach to the New World' of New York harbour, also by Norman Wilkinson, hung in the same place on the *Olympic*.

6

In the Wake of the Disaster

The *Mackay-Bennett* steamed out of Halifax harbour at 12.35p.m. on Wednesday 17 April 1912. The cable ship had been chartered by the White Star Line through its Halifax agents. Its mission was to search the area where the *Titanic* had sunk, and to recover any bodies they might find. On board there were several tons of ice, embalmer's tools and supplies, and a hundred plain wooden coffins. The largest undertaking firm in Nova Scotia, John Snow & Co., had been contracted, and they, in turn, asked for the assistance of every embalmer in the province. Captain F.H. Lardner supervised the loading, and Canon Hind, from Halifax's All Saint's Cathedral, was accompanying the expedition. The weather was cold and clear.

Soon after her departure, however, she was obliged to slow down because of fog, which cleared later in the day. On Friday, the fine weather gave way to rain and fog, which by evening had become very dense. The following day, the *Mackay-Bennett* sent wireless messages, requesting that any ship that had seen bodies or wreckage should contact her. A message was received from the German liner *Rhein* to say that they had spotted wreckage and bodies in latitude 42° 01' North, longitude 49° 13' West. The *Bremen* reported icebergs near the previous sighting. A cabin passenger on the *Bremen*, Mrs Stunke, described the scene from the liner's rail, as she and other passengers gazed out over the water:

It was between four and five o'clock on Saturday afternoon when we sighted an iceberg. The sun glistening upon it was a wonderful picture, but as we drew nearer, we could make out small dots floating in the sea, which we knew were the bodies of the Titanic's passengers. A feeling of awe and sadness crept over everyone. Approaching closer, we passed within 100 feet of the southernmost of the drifting wreckage, and, looking down, we distinctly saw a number of bodies so clearly that we could make out the clothing, and distinguish men from women. We saw one woman in her nightdress with a baby clasped closely to her breast. Several women passengers screamed at the sight, and left the rail in a fainting condition.

* * *

In the meantime, the *Carpathia*, carrying the survivors of the disaster, made a solemn entry into New York. The ship's progress had been hindered by the ice field and later by storms. Watching and waiting near the Cunard pier was a crowd of over 30,000, plus a further 10,000 along the Battery. At 8.00p.m. on Thursday evening, the *Carpathia* appeared out of the gloom.

* * *

The *Mackay-Bennett* arrived in the designated area late on Saturday. The following morning, cable engineer Frederick Hamilton, who kept a diary of the expedition, spotted two icebergs, the nearest being over 100ft high:

A solid mass of ice, against which the sea dashed furiously, throwing up geyser like columns of foam, high over the topmost summit, smothering the great mass at times completely in a cascade of spume as it pours over the snow and breaks into feathery crests on the polished surface of the berg ... which glints like a fairy building.

The ocean was strewn with wreckage: woodwork and deckchairs, as well as bodies. Whenever a group of bodies was sighted, a cutter would be lowered and the bodies hauled in, three or four at a time, before being taken aboard the cable ship. The saturated clothing made the work very difficult. Fifty-one bodies were recovered the first day, only four of them were women. The fourth body recovered was that of a little blonde-haired boy, about two years old. Members of the crew were deeply affected by this discovery.

On board, as each body was recovered, a piece of canvas with a stencilled number on it was attached. A description of each body (hair colour, height, approximate age and any distinguishing marks such as scars or birthmarks) was recorded in a ledger. Also recorded was an inventory of the objects found on the body. Any letters or passports were used to identify the bodies. All personal effects were placed in canvas bags, bearing the same number as the body.

At 8.15p.m., Canon Hind officiated at a burial service for the first of the recovered bodies, mostly crew, none of them identified, but all badly disfigured. Engineer Frederick Hamilton gave this account:

> The tolling of the bell summoned all hands to the forecastle where thirty bodies are to be committed to the deep, each carefully weighted and sewn up in canvas. It is a weird scene, this gathering. The crescent moon is shedding a faint light on us, as the ship lies wallowing in the great rollers. The funeral service is conducted by the Rev. Canon Hind; for nearly an hour, the words 'For as much as it has pleased … We therefore commit his body to the deep' are repeated, and at each interval comes Splash! as the weighted body plunges into the sea, there to sink to a depth of about two miles. Splash, splash, splash.

The recovery work resumed on Monday, when twenty-seven bodies were recovered from a sea strewn with enormous quantities of wreckage. Among the bodies was that of Colonel John Jacob Astor, whose body was badly crushed and there were soot marks on his face, which must have been a result of the falling funnel. One crewman remarked, 'Everybody had on a lifebelt, and bodies floated very high in the water in spite of sodden clothes and things in pockets.' However, some of them were 'very badly smashed and bruised' because of injuries sustained at the time of the sinking. All watches found on the bodies had stopped between 2.10 and 2.15a.m.

On Tuesday, the sea was dotted with bodies as far as the eye could see. The bodies, buoyed up by their lifejackets, had the appearance of 'a flock of gulls, at rest on the water.' The crew started their grim task at 6.30a.m. and, twelve hours later, 128 victims had been recovered: the decks were covered with bodies.

By Wednesday, supplies were severely depleted. There was a heavy sea and fog so dense that visibility was less than a ship's length, making further recovery operations virtually impossible. Cable Engineer Frederick Hamilton described the desolate conditions that prevailed that day: 'The hoarse tone of the steam whistle reverberating through the mist, the dripping rigging, and the ghostly sea, the heaps of dead …' He could not help but reflect on the dashed hopes of those whose loved ones had been wrenched from them by the tragedy.

The *Mackay-Bennett* cabled to the Allan Line RMS *Sardinian*, 'Recovering bodies of *Titanic*. Will be passing. Can you let us have all the canvas and burlap you can spare?' A few hours later, the two ships approached each other gingerly in the fog, and the trans-shipment was made. At this point, after another burial service, there were eighty bodies left on board.

*   *   *

Wireless reports continued to come in. The schooner *Banshee* reported a huge wreckage field, including, 'a considerable amount of white woodwork and framing.' Later, parts of the Grand Staircase were picked up, and it was noticed that most of the wreckage was from below deck.[1] At the time, it was assumed that an explosion had caused so much damage, but now we know for sure, after Robert Ballard's discovery of the *Titanic*, that the vessel broke in two as she sank.

Thursday proved to be another busy day for the crew, as eighty-seven more bodies were recovered. Captain Lardner sent a wireless message to the White Star offices in New York, 'All not embalmed will be buried at sea … Can only bring embalmed bodies to port,' He later explained that they 'came across the bodies in packs, looking like swimmers asleep.' In one group there had been a hundred bodies. Most of those recovered were found just on the edge of the Gulf Stream, which was to carry the remainder for many miles.[2]

As the *Mackay-Bennett*'s resources were so severely taxed, a second vessel, the *Minia*, was chartered. Her departure was delayed because there were not enough coffins available, but she finally set sail from Halifax just before midnight on Monday 22 April. She did not arrive at the disaster area until midnight on the 25th. Early next morning, after taking on board more embalming fluid, the *Mackay-Bennett* departed for Halifax. She had recovered 306 bodies, of which 116 had been buried at sea, being too badly decomposed to be brought to port. She returned with 190 of the recovered victims.

*   *   *

Meanwhile, in Dewsbury, Yorkshire, Wallace Hartley's parents were anxiously awaiting news of their son. The news of the disaster had made headlines all around the world on the 16th, but there was still a great deal of confusion and a general lack of reliable information. The *Daily Telegraph* published contradictory articles, reporting that the survivors, mainly women and children, were being brought back by the *Carpathia*, and that 'mystery surrounds the fate of the remainder'. However, another article in the same newspaper asserted that the *Titanic* was being towed to Halifax. A similar report appeared in the *Daily Mirror* too.

On the other side of the Atlantic, there were dramatic scenes as the news broke. A young naval officer wrote, in a letter dated 16 April:

> The terrible news about Titanic reached New York about 11p.m. last night, and the scene on Broadway was awful … the excitement was enough to cause a panic in the street…

The following day, incomplete lists of survivors appeared in the press, confirming that many of the crew and male passengers aboard had perished. The name of Wallace Hartley was missing from the lists.

Of the 1,500 who had gone into the sea on the night of the disaster, only the few who had managed to climb onto upturned collapsible B, or into a lifeboat, survived to return on the *Carpathia*, and some of those died of exposure before the rescue ship arrived.[3]

*   *   *

In a Salvation Army hostel in Kirkcudbright, Scotland, warden Captain Rex Sowden read the news about the *Titanic*. His thoughts immediately returned to the child whose hand he had held as she lay dying. In her delirium, she rambled about a disaster; there were people drowning and a man called Wally playing a 'fiddle'. It was the night the *Titanic* sank. Rex Sowden had known Wallace Hartley as a boy in Colne, but was unaware that he had gone to sea.

*   *   *

On Friday 19 April, the day after the *Carpathia* docked, the *New York Globe* carried the headline: 'Band Played "Nearer, My God, to Thee" as Ship Sank'.

On this side of the Atlantic, the *Daily Mirror* ran an article based on the testimony of a Miss Bonnell of Ohio, who stated that 'the orchestra belonging to the first cabin assembled on deck as the liner was going down and played *Nearer, My God, to Thee*.' These words would have struck a chord with Albion and Elizabeth Hartley, and we can only imagine their emotion as they heard the first real news of their son, knowing, as they did by now, that he was not among the survivors.

Ellwand Moody, Wallace's friend from Leeds, who, the day before the *Titanic*'s departure, had declined the invitation to sail with him, visited the Hartley home in Dewsbury the first week after the disaster. Mr Hartley was 'heart-broken'. He said to Ellwand Moody, 'Oh how I wish I could have taken his place.' During part of his subsequent interview with the press, Moody himself was in tears.

* * *

The world's press was looking for heroes, as well as answers as to why the tragedy had occurred. On 20 April, the *Daily Mirror* carried the headline, 'BAND GOES DOWN PLAYING'. Wallace Hartley and the other seven bandsmen were mentioned by name. There was a thumbnail biography of Wallace and a hurried sketch, which may have been copied from the only photograph available at the time.

In the days that followed, the heroism of the band captured the imagination of the country at large, and in many churches throughout the land, tributes were made to the *Titanic*'s dead, and one of the hymns frequently chosen was *Nearer, My God, to Thee*. In Washington, the hymn also opened the memorial service for Major Archibald Butt, President Taft's aide-de-camp. The President and his wife were present at the service.

* * *

In Smith Street, Colne, the home of the Lancaster family was bombarded with enquiries about their son, Seth, who was a cellist. The previous Christmas, he had been told he would be playing on the *Titanic*, but, near the time of sailing, he was transferred to the *Mauretania*, and he had left Liverpool the previous Saturday, taking Ellwand Moody's place.

* * *

While the *Minia* continued her search, preparations were being made in Halifax for the arrival of the *Mackay-Bennett*, which was expected the following Monday. The Mayflower Curling Rink was set up as a temporary morgue, where the coffins would be brought, and relatives would be able to identify their loved ones. Arrangements were made with railroad and shipping companies for the transport of coffins, and the American consul suspended the usual formalities governing the transfer of bodies to the United States. Relatives of the dead had already started to arrive and soon the hotels would be crowded. There was an air of expectancy in the town.

*   *   *

The *Leeds Mercury* continued to print articles regarding Wallace Hartley and the progress of the *Mackay-Bennett*. There was still no news as to whether the body of Wallace Hartley had been recovered.

Shoals of letters and telegrams were pouring into the Yorkshire home of Mr and Mrs Hartley. All paid tribute to the heroism of their son and offered condolences. Many referred to his selflessness in trying to cheer and comfort others when all was lost. The *Dewsbury Reporter* stated, 'His courage and calmness have touched the imagination of men and women in all parts of the world.' Mrs Hartley, pointing to a sheaf of 700 letters, said, 'These letters and telegrams cannot bring back my son, but they are a source of profound consolation to me.' She went on to say, 'My son was a good swimmer, but I know he would die clasping his violin. He was passionately attached to his instrument.'

*   *   *

The *Mackay-Bennett* had been delayed by storms, but, in the early morning of 30 April, she could be seen sailing past Chebucto Light, on her way into Halifax harbour, her flag fluttering at half-mast. On board was the body of Wallace Hartley.

On Saturday 27 April, Reuter's had released a list of recovered victims, and, on the 29th, under the headline 'YORKSHIRE HERO', the *Leeds Mercury* published the names. Halfway down was the name Wallace H. Hartley. The inclusion of the initial 'H', for Henry, left his parents in no doubt that this was, indeed, their son. Mr and Mrs Hartley were 'greatly affected by the news'.

OVER 200 BODIES RECOVERED.

(FROM OUR CORRESPONDENT.)

NEW YORK, APRIL 25.

The White Star Line have received the following wireless message, dated to-day, from the Mackay-Bennett :—

Bodies are numerous in latitude 41.35 north, longitude 48.37 west, extending many miles east and west. Mail ships should give this wide berth. Medical opinion is that death has been practically instantaneous in all cases owing to pressure when bodies went down in water. Drifting in dense fog since noon yesterday Total picked up 205. We brought away all embalming fluids to be had in Halifax, enough for seventy. With week fine weather think we would pretty well clear up relics of disaster. It is my opinion majority will never come surface.—MACKAY-BENNETT.

THE SIGHTING OF ICE.

Speaking at Falmouth yesterday SIR ERNEST SHACKLETON, referring to the loss of the Titanic, expressed a hope that those who conducted the British inquiry would be experts in their own particular branch of knowledge. For instance, the question as to the visibility of ice at night-time was most important. Many sailors knew, and especially those who were accustomed to navigation in ice-laden seas, that the higher above the deck a man was the less competent he was to judge of the approach of ice. He had his men as close to the water line as possible in misty weather and at night-time. When one was travelling near ice, an iceberg, if viewed from a high angle, would blend with the sea, whereas from the deck-line it would loom up on almost the darkest night.

A sub-committee of the Colne Town Council has decided to appeal for £500 for the purpose of erecting a memorial to Mr. Wallace Hartley, the conductor of the Titanic's band, who lost his life in the disaster. Mr. Hartley was a native of Colne.

A report (above) of the recovery of bodies by the *Mackay-Bennett*, and Wallace Hartley is listed among them (right).

RECOVERY OF THE BODIES.

MORE IDENTIFICATIONS.

(FROM OUR CORRESPONDENT.)

NEW YORK, APRIL 28.

The Mackay-Bennett is expected to arrive at Halifax to-morrow. The Minia is continuing the search. According to despatches, the Mackay-Bennett has recovered 219 bodies, of which 171 have been identified.

NEW YORK, APRIL 28.

The following additional bodies of those who perished in the Titanic disaster have been recovered by the Mackay-Bennett and identified :—

Amers Gustafson	E. Freeman
O. G. Ricks	R. Hengood
Pedro Ale	Maurice B. Debreneq
R. W. Leyson	W. Vanderhoof
Adolf Humblin	R. A. Waresam
F. Tamlyn	Frank D. Millet
Alfred Fellows	J. Hutchinson
Edward Lockyer	William Carter
W. Watson	Austin Vanbillard
F. Woodford	Leonard Rickman
Thomas Theobald	Edward A. Kert
M. Mayo	Owen G. Allum
Monroor Novel	Karvi Anderson
W. McQuillan	J. Story
M. Saunders	A. S. Nicholson
E. Price	H. Lyon
Thomas J. Everett	Pompio Piazzo
Mercia Hausea	J. Brown
Rossmore Abbott	F. Marsh
C. Shillabeer	E. G. Crosby
Petri Sempcrgnolos	A. Duewle
El. Gibbert	J. H. Coh
— D'Anbon	C. Milling
J. J. Davies	G. White
Alphonse Mrajff	S. Halloway
Clarke	Arthur Gee
G. Ingram	C. Gradisge
J. Ackerman	H. Jaillett
Alfred Roue	J. Reeves
Robert J. Bateman	Edward J. Rogers
Timothy McCarthy	S. Rantor
Alman Paulshon	Fred. Sawyer
Walter C. Porter	R. C. Belstow
Emil Branden	Waunree Buckly
Arthur D. McCrae	Denton Cox
George Lefevre	H. Y. Faunthorpe
Bernard I. Batiste	Ralph Gilca
S. Cove	Hans Givard
Aloniah Antania	Togail Hendekerio
Wallace H. Hartley	Gustaf Johanssoh
John S. March	Wentzell Linhart
T. Tewton	Thomas McAffry
J. Damon	Thomas Morgan
Dr. W. E. Minahan	Robert D. Norman
F. Roberts	— Pozzi
R. Saute	George Swane
Ergelharte Ostby	Welcario Sebastiano
T. F. Baxter	Leopold Weisz
Stanley H. Fox	Lauri Deracariah
Alfred King	

The Minia has recovered the bodies of :—

Sogurd Moen	A. Stanbrooke (steward)
Jacob Wiklund	Edward Elliott (fireman)

—*Reuter.*

*⁎*The spelling of the names is repeated as telegraphed.

⋆   ⋆   ⋆

The *Mackay-Bennett* sailed slowly into the harbour, which was unusually quiet and empty. All over the city, flags flew at half-mast. As the ship approached, the crew could be seen lining the rails. The coffins were piled on the stern, and a tarpaulin covered the hold. As the vessel docked at the Gun Wharf, men on shore doffed their hats. The only sound that could be heard was the melancholy tolling of the church bells.

The first man to set foot ashore was the embalmer, Mr John Snow. He told of the 'terribly mutilated condition of many of the bodies. Arms and legs were shattered, and faces and bodies mangled … There was evidence of a fierce struggle for life in some cases. Hands were clutching clothing, and faces were distorted with terror. Ours was a horrible task.'

The unloading began, and was to last almost three and a half hours. The first bodies to be brought ashore were crew who had not been embalmed. They were carried down from the foredeck to the wharf by the crew of the *Mackay-Bennett*. Next came the Second and Third Class passengers, for whom there were no coffins. Their remains had been stored in canvas bags in the ice-filled hold. Lastly the First Class passengers, all embalmed and in coffins, were taken down onto the wharf.

The recovered victims, borne on horse-drawn hearses, were taken in a grim procession up the steep route to the curling rink. Halifax was a city in deep mourning: black bunting was draped everywhere.

*   *   *

While all this was going on, Albion and Elizabeth Hartley were still in a state of suspense and anxiety. They knew that their son's body had been recovered from the Atlantic, but they still did not know whether he had been buried at sea or brought ashore. Mrs Hartley is reported to have said, 'If it is at all possible, we shall bring him home.'

The White Star Line had stated that they would help any families that wanted to have loved ones shipped home. Consequently, on Wednesday 1 May, Mr Hartley travelled to Liverpool to consult with Messrs Black, the music agents for the White Star Line. He returned without any definite news. The following day, therefore, he cabled to Halifax.

Maria Robinson was also awaiting news. With wording that would appeal to the stiff upper-lipped readers of the day, the headline ran, 'Bereaved Fiancée Bearing up Bravely'.

*   *   *

At the Mayflower Curling Rink relatives had been waiting anxiously. As the first coffins were brought into the darkened building, a quiet descended. Those victims who had been embalmed at sea were placed reverently in the main rink; the others were taken behind a curtain where embalmers were waiting to start their work. Once all the coffins were in place, the viewing could begin.

News soon arrived from Halifax to the effect that Wallace's body had been brought ashore. Albion Hartley did not need to join the dozens of relatives in the Mayflower Curling Rink. Wallace Hartley had been identified, and Albion was satisfied. It was not the violin case strapped to the body that had identified him, but various possessions that were now in a canvas bag marked No. 224.

The record of Wallace Hartley's body and effects reads thus:

No. 224   Male   Estimated age, 25   Hair, Brown

CLOTHING – Uniform (green facing); brown overcoat; black
     boots; green socks.
EFFECTS – Gold fountain pen, "W.H.H."; diamond solitaire
     ring; silver cigarette case; letters; silver match box, marked "To
     W.H.H. from Collingson's staff, Leeds"; telegram to Hotley,
     Bandmaster "Titanic", nickel watch; gold chain; gold cigar
     holder; stud; scissors; 16s.; 16 cents; coins.

BANDMASTER WALLACE H. HOTLEY (sic)

The green socks may have been a uniform requirement as at least one other musician had been wearing them. Mr Foulds, Elizabeth Hartley's brother, received a letter from the family, informing him that they were satisfied as to the identification of their son.

It is not known who sent the telegram found on the body; perhaps it was Maria, who had missed seeing him before he left. Of the letters found on the body, one was from Wallace's parents, the other, water-stained but still legible, was from a friend in Egremont, on the Wirral, dated 9 April:

My Dear Wallace,
Am very sorry I missed you. I waited at the end of Brooke's Alley and got to Byrom's just after you had left. Jolly good luck, old chap. Would give more than a trifle to be with you. Don't forget to drop me a line at 61, Lea Road.
     Bon Voyage and Bon [sic] Santé,
     Bill.[5]

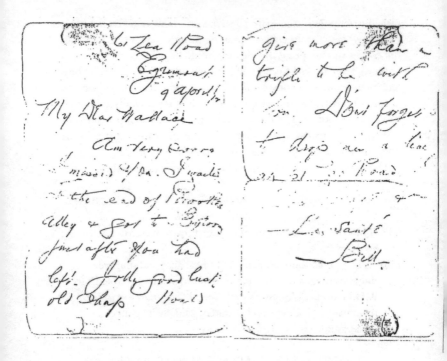

The water-stained letter that was found on Wallace Hartley's body.

The words he had written must have been ringing in his ears as news of the tragedy unfolded.

On 3 May, there began a series of burials at the Fairview Cemetery in Halifax. At 3.00p.m. a service started which ended with the hymn *Nearer, My God, to Thee*, played by the Royal Canadian Regiment. Fifty victims of the disaster were laid to rest. In all, 150 of those recovered would remain in Halifax in its hallowed ground. The *Minia*, which was on her way home, added only a further seventeen victims to the list.

The following day there was only one funeral, that of the little blonde-haired boy, whose tragic death had touched the hearts of the crew and public alike, especially when no one came forward to claim his body. His white coffin, bedecked with flowers, was borne by six sailors from the *Mackay-Bennett*. The crew of the cable ship later paid for a gravestone.[6]

Among those buried in Halifax were Wallace Hartley's fellow bandsmen, Jock Hume, who was buried at Fairview on 8 May, and Frederick Clarke from Liverpool, buried on the same day, whose grave is at the Mount Olivet Catholic Cemetery. All three musicians may have stayed together at the end and been found together, as their numbers were quite close together (No.193, No.202 and No.224). But Wallace Hartley was not going to be buried alongside them: on 2 May instructions had been given via the New York offices of the White Star Line. Wallace was going home.

Wallace's body had been embalmed, and, because it had been identified, it was taken to the undertaker's. It was now placed in a casket ready for the next stage of its long journey.

*   *   *

With regard to the effects of recovered bodies, arrangements were made between the American consul Ragsdale and the Hon. G.H. Murray, Premier of Nova Scotia. In the absence of any treaty between Great Britain and the United States, the Premier agreed to arrange and facilitate the transfer of personal effects to relatives. All the numbered canvas bags were kept in the coroner's office in Halifax until their release was authorised. The violin case, which, according to newspaper reports, was to be forwarded to the White Star Line, did not feature on the list. On 2 May, the *Acadian Reporter*, *Evening Echo* and *Evening Mail*, all Canadian newspapers, contained articles regarding Wallace Hartley's effects. The articles reported that, when the bundle of effects was opened, it included his music case and continued: '*This will be forwarded to New York with his uniform and other clothing found on the body.*'

This report appeared in the *Yorkshire Post*, dated Tuesday 30 April.

MR WALLACE HARTLEY'S BODY RECOVERED.
Halifax (Nova Scotia). Thursday.
The body of Wallace hartley, the heroic Bandmaster of the 'Titanic',
was positively identified last night, and his music case was strapped to
him. This will be forwarded to the White Star Company.

Some effects were retained by the Provincial Secretary for the Province of Nova Scotia, whose office was in Halifax. To obtain these effects, it was necessary to send certified copies of letters of administration to the said Secretary. However, in the case of Wallace

Hartley (as well as many of the other recovered bodies), this was not necessary, as arrangements were made on behalf of the Hartley family, and Wallace's effects were transferred into the possession of the White Star Line. Nova Scotia Archives have suggested that the violin was returned to the fiancée. This would explain why it was not included in the items to be returned to Albion Hartley.

The nearest port from which the White Star Line operated a transatlantic service was Boston. On 4 May, the casket containing Wallace Hartley's body was put on a train bound for Boston and was carried by rail the several hundred miles to the port. Here it was transferred to the White Star liner *Arabic*, which set sail early on the morning of Tuesday 7 May, bound for Liverpool.[7] The journey was due to last approximately ten days.

On 8 May, the news was announced that the Hartley family was making arrangements for Wallace to be buried in the family grave in his home town of Colne. His two infant brothers were already buried there, and the Hartley family had numerous relatives in the town.

Albion Hartley now had the painful task of making the final arrangements for his son's burial. To this purpose, he travelled to Colne on Saturday 11 May, and conferred with the undertaker, Mr J. Ridehalgh, and also the Mayor, Councillor Turner Hartley JP (no relation), on behalf of Colne Corporation. It had been decided that this heroic son of Colne would be given a civic funeral, which would take place the following Saturday.

The *Arabic* was due in Liverpool on Friday 17 May in the early morning. The undertaker would be on the quayside when the vessel docked, and would convey the body directly to Colne. Albion Hartley would also be on the quayside, waiting for his son.

Endnotes

1　Some of the wreckage is now on view in the Maritime Museum in Halifax, including a deckchair and a piece of panelling with beautiful carvings, copied for Cameron's film *Titanic* and used as the piece of wreckage that Rose climbed onto. Discovered on the debris field by salvage teams were the metal parts of the stringed instruments.

2　There is a sharp dividing line between the Labrador Current and the Gulf Stream, with a thin bank of mist running along it, which has been likened to a 'magic curtain'.

3　Second Officer Charles Lightoller, Colonel Archibald Gracie, Assistant Wireless Operator Harold Bride, Jack Thayer and baker Charles Joughin, among others. Jack Phillips had also found his way onto the raft, but died during the night. Rosa Abbott climbed into collapsible A.

4   The metal parts of the stringed instruments found on the debris field did not include the violin belonging to Wallace Hartley, as this was in the case strapped to his body.

5   Bill's exact identity is unknown, but he must have known Wallace very well to know of his routine and transfer to the *Titanic*. He was probably one of the musicians' fraternity. The head of household at 61 Tea Road, John Young McLeod, was a maker of nautical instruments, another connection with the sea. The letter, along with the one from Wallace's parents, was auctioned by Sotheby's on 20 July 1981, but did not reach the reserve price. The last letters written by Wallace to his parents (posted in Reading and Queenstown) were sold on the same occasion to a man in Toronto for £1,300.

6   The favourite theory is that the unknown child was Gosta Leonard Palsson from Sweden, whose mother and siblings also died in the sinking. Other *Titanic* experts believe him to be the three-year-old Eugene Rice from Ireland whose mother, Margaret, was found close by on the first day, whereas Mrs Palsson's body was found a great distance away.

7   White Star liner *Arabic*, maiden voyage Liverpool-New York, 1903. Transferred to Liverpool-Boston route, 1905. Torpedoed and sunk 19 August 1915 by U-boat off the Old Head of Kinsale, outward bound with twenty-six Americans on board. This is one of the incidents, as well as that of the more significant sinking of the *Lusitania*, which drew the USA into the First World War. Like the *Titanic*, and all ships of the White Star Line, the name of the ship ended with the letters -ic.

7

The Homecoming

On the landing stage at Liverpool, the crowd was still waiting. It was a lovely morning with a slight nip in the air. The RMS *Arabic* had been due to dock at 7.15a.m., but this was later extended to 8.30a.m. The river was already busy with tugs and vessels. Seagulls flapped around noisily.

Albion Hartley was also on the quayside. He had travelled from Colne to await the arrival of his son. One cannot presume to know the thoughts that were going through his head, but it must have occurred to him, as he stood there waiting endlessly, that it was only a matter of weeks (or perhaps he was counting in days, hours, minutes), since his son had walked here, having just disembarked from the *Mauretania*. How very different was this homecoming.

It was approaching 10.00a.m. as the *Arabic* loomed up in sight by the Rock Light. Her progress towards her moorings was agonisingly slow. For those alighting, there were joyous embraces, as friends and family members were reunited, but, in the words of a native of Colne who witnessed the scene:

> There was a father there to meet his son; but, oh! under what different conditions! No loving, fond embrace for him; no hearty grip of the hand; no kiss on the cheek; all that remained of the boy of his heart was encased in a leaden shell. The ruthless sea had claimed him …

Later in the day, after all the passengers had alighted, the *Arabic* was moved to her berthage at the west end of the South Canada Dock. The shed, opposite to where the liner had been moored, was roped off from the public. Only some White Star officials, the undertakers' staff and a limited number of Pressmen were allowed to be present, as well as relatives. One of the Black brothers, music directors for the

White Star Line, was probably also present, as he would later have a prominent place at the funeral.

Three hearses were standing by; one had come to Liverpool by road from Colne, drawn by horses. Three coffins were brought ashore. One contained the body of a First Class Saloon steward by the name of Arthur Lawrence, aged thirty-five years, whose body tag had borne the number No.90. He was near the end of his journey, as he would be buried at West Derby Cemetery in Liverpool. The second coffin belonged to a Third Class passenger, Owen George Allum, eighteen, who had boarded the *Titanic* at Southampton, on his way to New York to meet up with his father. He would be buried at Clewer Parish Churchyard, Windsor, on 22 May. The third coffin was that of Wallace Hartley.

Wallace Hartley's father was waiting to sign the receipt of delivery of the effects. In addition to the effects listed previously, there was the 'insignia cut from uniform' i.e. the White Star lapel badges. The receipt was on headed notepaper from the White Star Line offices, New York.[1] According to those present, Albion was 'much affected'. His hand trembled as he wrote his signature.

The casket was in the American style, made of polished wood that looked like mahogany to some, rosewood to others, with heavy brass mountings. Inside this outer shell, the remains were enclosed in a plain, wooden airtight case, lined with tin. As is usual with American caskets, part of the lid could be opened to reveal the face of the deceased beneath a glass panel. When this was done, it was immediately apparent that the body was that of Wallace Hartley, although the features had a greenish tinge due to the embalming fluid and the length of time spent in the water. Like so many other victims of the disaster, Wallace had received an injury during the sinking, there being the mark of a blow to his face. Albion Hartley had the official task of identifying his son.

The casket was placed in the hearse, ready for departure. It was approximately 3.00p.m. in the afternoon when all the formalities were complete, and the journey back to Colne began. The sixty-mile journey took ten hours to complete. Throughout the night, the hearse made its way back to the town on the hill, and finally arrived at 1.00a.m. the following morning.

At the Bethel Chapel in Colne, where Wallace had been a chorister and Albion had been choirmaster, there was a group of about twenty awaiting the arrival of the hearse. Mrs Hartley was

AMERICAN LINE
ATLANTIC TRANSPORT LINE
DOMINION LINE
LEYLAND LINE
RED STAR LINE
WHITE STAR LINE
WHITE STAR-DOMINION LINE

PASSENGER DEPARTMENT

9 BROADWAY

NEW YORK

RE. S. S. "TITANIC":   TRIPLICATE:

      I hereby solemnly state that I am lawfully entitled
to take possession of all the personal effects in your hands
taken from the body of MR. WALLACE H. HARTLEY,   a
passenger on the "Titanic", and in consideration of the delivery
to me of said effects, without production of letters testa-
mentary or of administration, I agree to indemnify and save
harmless the White Star Line against the claims of any person
on account of said effects.

      I acknowledge receipt of the following effects:

Gold fountain pen, "W.H.H."
Diamond solitaire ring,
Silver cigarette case,
Letters,
Silver match box, marked "To W.H.H. from Collingson's
      staff, Leeds,"
Telegram to Hartley, Bandmaster "Titanic,"
Nickel watch, gold chain,
Gold cigar holder,
Stud,
Scissors,
16 sh. 16 d., coins, also 21 cts., 2 Francs, 1/2 Mark,
Key,
Insignia cut from uniform.

WITNESS:

John Moore.

Albion Hartley's signature can be seen clearly in this receipt of his son's effects. From 'Coroner's Report, Body #224, Mr Wallace Hartley'; in NSARM RG 41, Series A, Vol. 76A. (Nova Scotia Archives and Record Management)

not present among them, as she would arrive by train the following morning with her daughters and Wallace's fiancée, Maria Robinson.[2] The casket was borne into the chapel, where it would remain all night, and was placed on a purple-draped bier in front of the pulpit. It now bore the inscription, which had been plated in Colne:

WALLACE H. HARTLEY,
Died April 15th, 1912,
Aged 33 years.

'Nearer My God To Thee'

In the light of day, Wallace's father, mother and other close relatives, as well as his fiancée, came to have a last look at their loved one. It was a pathetic sight. Grouped round the coffin, they gazed for several minutes, and it was with great difficulty that they tore themselves away. Then the coffin lid was screwed down for the last time.

Later, other relatives and members of the public were allowed in to pay their respects. They filed past all morning in a steady stream. Floral tributes were piled high in front of the pulpit. Among them was one from the restaurant St James in Manchester and another from the Amalgamated Musicians' Union: 'A token of respect and admiration'.

The grief-stricken father said to one sympathiser, 'We are very proud of my son, but that does not fill the place he has left. It was a fine thing he did, I know, but I am more sad than proud.'

As 1.00p.m. approached, the thoroughfares near the chapel became congested with people gathering to get a good view. When the civic procession from the Town Hall arrived, there were several hundred people gathered outside the chapel. The police had to make way for the family and other mourners to pass through. A congregation of 1,000 was waiting inside the building, which, in normal circumstances, could only accommodate 700.

Inside the chapel, the gallery and sides were thronged with members of the public. In the central area, the front pew was occupied by Mr and Mrs Hartley, their daughters, Lizzie and Hilda, and Maria Robinson. Nearby, the casket lay on a catafalque, surrounded with flowers, their heavy scent filling the air.

The service began with an organ voluntary by Mendelssohn, followed by hymns, prayers and an address by Mr Thomas Worthington, an independent Methodist preacher, who was a friend of Wallace's father. During his rather lengthy sermon, he mentioned that, on a trip across the Atlantic aboard the *Mauretania*, he had been approached by Wallace, who remembered him from his boyhood.

Throughout the service, Mr and Mrs Hartley were overcome with emotion. Wallace's father was bent, his brow furrowed with care and sorrow. He was shaking visibly, and could scarcely take his eyes off the coffin. When the rest of the congregation stood to sing the hymns, Wallace's mother remained seated, sobbing bitterly and choking back her tears. Towards the end of the service, the Colne Orchestral Society began to play *Nearer, My God, to Thee.* The singing began, but trailed off, as many people were unable to continue. 'Scarcely a soul in the church but shed tears as the hymn was sung.'

As the mourners were about to leave the chapel, Maria Robinson rose from her seat, picked up her wreath, a cross of red roses, and placed it over the brass plate on the casket. The wreath bore the words, 'Teach me from my heart to say "Thy will be done."' Wallace's two younger sisters then placed their wreaths over his head and feet.

Outside, a procession half a mile long was forming. There were bands from all the neighbouring towns: Nelson, Brierfield, Haggate, Trawden and the 5th Battalion East Lancashire Regiment from Burnley, as well as buglers, scouts and representatives of various bodies and organisations, including the Amalgamated Musicians' Union. Boys clung to the railings and stood on stone pillars to get a better view.

As the casket was borne out of the chapel on the shoulders of twelve pall-bearers, eight of them Wallace's cousins, the bands, with muffled drums, began to play the Dead March in 'Saul'. They would continue all the way to the cemetery. The casket was placed on the horse-drawn hearse and the procession moved off, to the slow rhythm of the music.

At the head of the procession were four mounted police, followed by a body of thirty policemen on foot. Behind them marched the bands, with the Colne Band in the lead. The Mayor of Colne, the Town Clerk and members of the Town Council walked behind. The first of the carriages was occupied by Mr Worthington and Mr Black from the music agency in Liverpool, who may have been representing the White Star Line.[3] Behind came the hearse, followed by a landau carrying flowers. Wallace's parents with his two younger sisters rode in the next carriage, and behind them were Maria Robinson and the family of Wallace's eldest sister, Mary.

There were six other carriages carrying relatives. Most of the ladies, including Margaret Hartley, a cousin of Wallace's, were wearing the wide-brimmed hats that were fashionable at the time; Margaret later remembered that they had to tilt their heads to allow the hats through the carriage doors.[4] At the rear of the procession came the Mayor's carriage, which was occupied by the Mayoress.

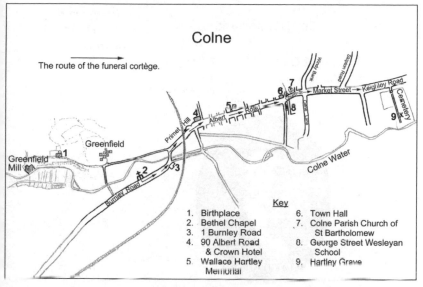

Colne as it was when the Hartleys lived there. The arrows show the route of the funeral procession through the town from Bethel Chapel to the cemetery.

The cortège made its way slowly along the main thoroughfare of the town, down Burnley Road, past No.1 on the right, where the family had lived for several years, up Primet Hill and into Albert Road.

On the left, just after the Crown Hotel was No.90, where the family had lived for five years before leaving Colne in 1895.

By now an estimated crowd of 30,000 – greater than the population of the town – lined the streets, many of them mill-workers, who had hurried home to get changed out of their work clothes. There was an element of curiosity among the people who watched, but also genuine sympathy. People had travelled from the neighbouring towns as well as Dewsbury and Leeds. Among the crowd were three survivors of the disaster, a stewardess and two crew-members, who had travelled by car from London, and who would leave discreetly afterwards. Along the route, all curtains were drawn as a mark of respect. Men doffed their hats as the hearse passed by, and women wept unashamedly. Colne had never witnessed such a scene.

In Memoriam: A
Wallace Hartley
memorial card.
(Darran Ward).

The procession continued its journey up Albert Road, to the top of the hill where it passed the impressive Town Hall building, whose architect had also designed the Town Hall in Manchester. The cortège then moved into Church Street, past the ancient parish church of Saint Bartholomew,[5] along Market Street with its stone market cross. The procession had followed the main route through the town, and was now on Keighley Road, approaching the town cemetery. Wallace Hartley's final journey covered about a mile and a quarter and had taken an hour.

The cemetery in Colne is situated on a hillside, overlooked by another hill, dotted with farms and cattle. The general atmosphere is one of peace and serenity.

The procession moved down the steep hillside, past the Foulds family grave, where members of Mrs Hartley's family are buried. The police and bandsmen formed a cordon round the open grave,

1 A modern view of Colne, which has changed little since Wallace Hartley lived here, showing the Town Hall (centre top). The large building just below is the Wesleyan school that Wallace attended.

2 Left: 92 Greenfield Road (formerly Hill) – Wallace Hartley's birthplace.

3 Below: The row of cottages on Greenfield Road where Wallace Hartley was born, showing Pendle Hill in the background.

4 Above: George Street Wesleyan School, attended by Wallace Hartley.

5 Left: 90 Albert Road, Colne. The family lived here from 1890–1895.

6 Below: 1 Burnley Road, Colne, the Hartley residence from 1885–1887. The house is at the end of the row, next to the post office.

7 *Above:* Wallace Hartley, aged fifteen. (*Nelson Leader*)

8 *Above right:* Wallace Hartley, aged seventeen, around the time that the family left Colne. (*Colne Times*)

9 *Right:* A portrait of Wallace Hartley in his later years. (*Burnley Express*)

10 Left: 35 Somerset Road, the Hartley family home in the Almondbury area of Huddersfield, 1895–1902.

11 Right: Hillcrest Avenue, Leeds.

12 'Surreyside', West Park Street, Dewsbury.

13 Dewsbury, where the Hartley family lived at the time of the tragedy. In the background is the Town Hall, where two concerts were held on 12 and 19 May 1912 to raise funds for a memorial.

14 The Kursaal, Harrogate, opened 1903, where Wallace Hartley played early in his career. (From the collection of the late Jean Elizabeth Martin)

15 Prince's Parade, Bridlington, with the Floral Pavilion to the left and Grand Pavilion ahead.

16 The Floral Pavilion, Royal Prince's Parade, Bridlington, showing the band on the bandstand.

17 Edwardian ladies and gentlemen strolling along Prince's Parade, Bridlington. The Floral Pavilion on the left show shows the bandstand. In the background is the Grand Pavilion, where a memorial concert was held for the *Titanic* musicians.

18 The band inside the Floral Pavilion. Wallace Hartley is fourth from left in the front row, holding his violin. (By courtesy of East Riding of Yorkshire Information Services)

19 The bandstand, Roundhay Park, Leeds. Wallace played at Roundhay during his early career.

20 *Above:* Collinson's Orient Café façade, King Edward Street.

21 *Right:* The interior of the Jigsaw shop in King Edward Street, Leeds, which used to be Collinson's Café. The building has been restructured to be as it was originally, showing the elliptical well and dome. (By kind permission of Jenny O'Hara McRandal of Jigsaw)

22 Briggate, Leeds, showing the complex of buildings now called the Victoria Quarter. King Edward Street, site of Collinson's Café, runs between the two turrets. (Darran Ward).

23 The Boat House (formerly the Spa Rooms), Boston Spa, where Hartley and his fiancée Maria went boating.

24 *Above left:* An Edwardian violinist plays to his audience and thinks of his sweetheart. With his long, dark hair, he bears a fleeting resemblance to Wallace Hartley.
25 *Above right:* Soprano Fanny Moody, who, with husband Charles Manners, founded the Moody-Manners Opera Company.

26 *Above left:* Charles Manners, baritone, who had been a member of the Carl Rosa Opera Company and married Fanny Moody in 1890. (Darran Ward)
27 *Above right:* Carl Rosa, who founded the famous opera company which still performs today. Wallace Hartley joined the company before going to sea.

28 A 1911 view of the New York skyline, as Wallace Hartley would have seen it. (From the collection of the late Jean Elizabeth Martin)

29 Times Square, New York. This too would have been a familiar sight for Wallace Hartley. (From the collection of the late Jean Elizabeth Martin)

30 The Liver Building, completed in 1911, as it was when Wallace Hartley used to disembark from the *Mauretania* in Liverpool, before the Cunard building was erected.

31 The *Mauretania* at the Landing Stage, Liverpool, facing the mouth of the Mersey. (From the collection of the late Jean Elizabeth Martin)

32 RMS *Lusitania* at sea. Built by John Brown & Co. at Clydebank, she was the fastest ship on the Atlantic until she lost the Blue Riband to her sister ship, the *Mauretania*.

33 The *Lusitania* at the Landing Stage, Liverpool. She can be distinguished from her sister ship, the *Mauretania*, because the air vents on her boat deck are less prominent, and the 'portholes' below the bridge are round, as opposed to oblong.

34 The *Lusitania* at Chelsea Piers, New York. This was pier #54; *Titanic* would have docked at pier #59. (Darran Ward)

35 RMS *Mauretania* at sea. It was said of her, 'She had the manners and deportment of a great lady and behaved herself as such.'

36 *Mauretania* at the Landing Stage, Liverpool. Her more prominent air vents and oblong 'portholes' below the bridge are noticeable.

37 *Mauretania* arriving at Cherbourg. *Titanic*, too, called at Cherbourg before continuing her journey across the Atlantic. The Astors and Molly Brown boarded here.

38 Mauretania's Verandah Café.

39 Mauretania leaving New York. Wallace Hartley sailed past the Statue of Liberty many times while on board the great ship.

40 *Left:* The St James building in Oxford Street, Manchester. Built next to the Palace Theatre, it was completed in 1912. Wallace Hartley played in the restaurant here when *Mauretania* was in dock. The management of the restaurant sent a wreath to Colne for Wallace's funeral.

41 *Below:* Church Street, Liverpool. The shop of the violin maker Byrom's was located just off here. Fred Clarke, the bass player, played at the Kardomah Café at the far end on the right.

42 Above; Liverpool Town Hall, close to the Cunard offices at Water Street. This view of Castle Street shows No.14 (the second building from the left) where C.W. and F.N. Black had their office on the third floor.

43 Right: The White Star building, Liverpool. It is said Bruce Ismay had an office in the turret.

44 The great gantries, Harland & Wolff shipyard, Belfast. Both *Titanic* and her sister ship *Olympic* were built here.

SOUTHAMPTON DOCKS, FROM THE AIR.   91392.

45 The *Olympic* at the White Star dock in Southampton. This is where *Titanic* sailed from on 10 April 1912.

46 The White Star wharf, Queenstown. *Titanic* called here before continuing across the Atlantic. (From the collection of the late Jean Elizabeth Martin)

47 *Titanic*'s sister ship *Olympic* entering New York harbour. (From the collection of the late Jean Elizabeth Martin)

48 *Above: Titanic* passing Hythe pier sailing down from Southampton. A rare view of the *Titanic* and one of the last glimpses of the ship. (By courtesy of the University of Liverpool Library, D.175/2)

49 *Right:* Although entitled 'RMS *Titanic*', the picture shows her sister ship *Olympic.* The upper deck of *Titanic* was glazed in, making her only marginally heavier and, therefore, the biggest liner in the world. (Darran Ward)

50 Left: The 'Unsinkable' Molly Brown heard the music of the ship's orchestra as her lifeboat drifted away from the sinking ship.

51 Below: The deck band of the *Kaiserin Auguste Victoria* playing the morning concert. (*Musical America,* 7 May 1912)

52 *Above:* Lifeboats flee
as *Titanic* sinks.

53 *and* 54 *Titanic*
prior to her iceberg
collision.

55 Halifax harbour, Nova Scotia. The bodies recovered from the North Atlantic were brought here on board the *Mackay-Bennett* and the *Minia*.

56 'CS *Minia*/Recovering one of the bodies'; in NSARM Photo Collection: Transportation & Communication: Ships & Shipping. (Nova Scotia Archives and Record Management)

57 *Opposite above:* 'CS *Minia*/Embalming work in progress'; in NSARM Photo Collection: Transportation & Communication: Ships & Shipping. (Nova Scotia Archives and Record Management)

58 The bodies arrive back at Halifax to be transported to the Mayflower Curling Rink. 'CS *Minia*/Landing the bodies at Halifax'; in NSARM Photo Collection: Transportation & Communication: Ships & Shipping. (Nova Scotia Archives and Record Management)

59 The *Arabic*, which brought Wallace Hartley's body back to Liverpool from Boston.

60 Wallace Hartley's coffin being carried out of the Bethel Chapel. (Darran Ward)

61 The funeral procession making its way through Colne towards the cemetery. (Darran Ward)

62 Mourners at the funeral, showing Albion Hartley on the extreme right. (Darran Ward)

63 The Outward Bound, 1912 (oil on canvas) by Frederick Cayley-Robinson, (1862-1927). (Leeds Museums and Galleries (City Art Gallery) UK/The Bridgeman Art Library)

64 Titanic musicians' memorial, Southampton. (Photo Brian Burnell)

65 Wallace Hartley's grave in Colne Cemetery.

66 The Hartley memorial in Colne.

67 Detail from Wallace Hartley's grave.

68 Left: Detail, Wallace Hartley memorial, Colne. (From the collection of the late Jean Elizabeth Martin)

69 Below: Titanic concert held in 2002 at Colne Municipal Hall, showing Jonathan Evans-Jones, who played Wallace in the film, wearing his *Titanic* costume. On the extreme left, in Edwardian dress, is the late Jean Elizabeth Martin, to whom this book is dedicated. (Published by kind permission of East Lancashire Newspapers)

which was lined with lilies of the valley and other spring flowers. The last rites were pronounced. Then, as the coffin was lowered into the ground, the Bethel Choir sang, *Nearer, My God, to Thee.*

To close the ceremony, a small band of scout buglers sounded the 'Last Post'. The notes went floating through the valley, echoing among the hills, before dying out …

And, high above, a lark sang.

Endnotes

1   No.9 Broadway. The receipt indemnified the White Star Line against any
     claims regarding the said effects.
2   Mrs Hartley left Dewsbury on the 9.08a.m. train with her daughters
     Lizzie and Hilda, to be joined in Huddersfield by daughter Mary, who was
     accompanied by her husband. Maria Robinson will have boarded the train at
     Leeds.
3   No initials supplied. It is not known whether this was C.W. or F.N. Black.
4   Margaret Hartley was the daughter of Albion's brother, John Rushton. Years
     later, she related details of the funeral to her daughter. She had seen Wallace's
     face through the glass panel of the casket, and noted the discolouration of the
     skin.
5   Several generations of the author's family were baptised, married and buried
     here, dating back to 1716.

8

Nearer, My
God, to Thee

The image of the band going down playing the hymn, *Nearer, My God, to Thee*, captured the imagination of the whole world. Newspapers throughout the world carried headlines and ran articles about the heroic bandsmen. The music and words of the hymn filled the whole of the front page of the *Daily Mirror* a few days after the disaster. The favourite hymn of the late King Edward VII, it was being played up and down the country at memorial services and concerts. In Washington, it was sung at a service for Archibald Butt, President Taft's aide-de-camp: the President himself was in the congregation. At the end of April, it was sung in Paris by the 250-strong choir from Leeds.

The *London Standard* had this to say:

> We are usually an undemonstrative people, but the incident of the string band[1] of the Titanic, its members gathered together to play the hymn, 'Nearer, My God, to Thee', as the great ship settled for her last plunge, left men speechless with pity. It is a great incident in history.

Reports became increasingly exaggerated, in a style which is no longer appreciated. The account of Mrs A.A. Dick had become further embellished since her first report: 'The last I remember of the *Titanic* was hearing the strains of *Nearer, My God, to Thee*. Then there was a great rushing of water and the vessel sank beneath the waves.'

Mrs John Murray Brown (not to be confused with Molly Brown) declared: 'The last I saw of the band, the musicians were up to their knees in water.' A grossly exaggerated account.

One of the cabled interviews describes the scene thus:

Suddenly the band stopped; the leader moved his baton, and, in slow, solemn tones, the air Nearer, My God, to Thee was wafted across the water to our ears. The band played the hymn continuously until their instruments were choked off by the swirling water that closed about their heads as they went to a hero's grave.[2]

A 1950s film of the disaster (not the highly regarded *A Night to Remember*) showed the men remaining on board lined against the rail singing the hymn along with the band.

It was reported in a newspaper article printed in May 1912 that a medium had a 'conversation' with William Stead, a journalist who was famous at the time and who had perished in the disaster. He allegedly affirmed that he had asked the band to play *Nearer, My God, to Thee*.

Soon, poems and songs were being written on both sides of the Atlantic. One American title was *The Band Played Nearer, My God, to Thee as the Ship Went Down*, penned by Mark Beam and Harold Jones. *The Band was Playing as the Ship went down*, was written and composed by Robert Donnelly. The following lines are from a poem written at the time:

> Over the waiting, starlit sea,
> Trembled the song of devotion.
> The song of the souls that all would be
> 'Nearer, My God, to Thee',
> There on the lonely ocean.

Joseph Conrad, the celebrated author, who had spent much of his life at sea, spoke scathingly of this kind of sentimentality. He referred to the now famous hymn as 'Music to get drowned by'. He continued by saying: 'It would have been finer if the band of the *Titanic* had been quietly saved, instead of being drowned while playing – whatever the tune they were playing, the poor devils...'

Even in France, the notion of the band playing the hymn up to the last moment attracted so much attention that a cheap edition of a French translation was published, and, in less than a week, 50,000 copies were sold at the equivalent of a penny each. *Plus près de Toi, Mon Dieu* was being sung by groups of people on street corners, after the manner of popular songs.

No.137 in the White Star Line Music Book, *Songe d'Automne*, was one of the songs played in the ship's last few hours. (Courtesy of International Music Publications Limited)

Although people did not necessarily believe that the band played with the water swirling round their feet, as some reports asserted, it was generally accepted that the hymn was played, and people everywhere took the hymn to their hearts.

But there were voices, albeit tiny ones, against this blind acceptance. A group of women from First Class asserted that they 'never saw nor heard the band'. Although they boarded a lifeboat on port side, they may have spent some time on starboard, as they remembered seeing First Officer Murdoch, who was in charge of loading on that side of the ship.

Colonel Archibald Gracie, in a lecture he gave at University Club in Washington on 23 November 1912, two weeks before he died, stated that the band stopped playing half an hour before the ship sank. He did not include this information in his book, *The Truth about Titanic*. It is a mystery why he changed his story: his book is a highly regarded account of his own experience.

Similarly, Algernon H. Barkworth, a First Class passenger from Hull, who was on board until near the end, said, 'I do not wish to detract from the bravery of anybody, but …' He continued to say that the band had been playing a waltz when he first went onto the deck, but later, when he passed the same place, 'they had thrown down their instruments and were not to be seen.' According to an article printed in *The Times*, he would 'never forget the fierce jarring notes of that waltz'. At some point the band may have had to search for their lifejackets, as they put these on during the course of the evening, but it is extremely doubtful that Wallace Hartley would have abandoned his violin, even momentarily, on the deck of a sinking ship.

The above are in the minority. There are too many people who heard the band playing till the end to try to assert otherwise. At the British Inquiry, chaired by Lord Mersey, Steward Edward Brown was asked:

'Do you know what the band were doing at the last?'

'I do not remember hearing the band stop playing. They were playing for a long time, but I do not remember hearing them stop.'

'Were they playing at the time when you were dealing with this collapsible boat from the top of the officers' quarters?'

'Yes.'

'Up to as late as that your memory serves you?'

'Yes, they were playing then.'

'Do you mean up to the time when the Captain called out to you to look after the women and children?'

'Yes, they were playing a few seconds before that, Sir.'

The people in boats, who had the leisure to sit and listen, certainly heard the band playing. The others, because of the dramatic circumstances, can be forgiven for not paying attention.

There is no doubt, therefore, that the band played to the end. More difficult to determine is what they actually played. Archibald Gracie was adamant that no hymns were played, although, as we know, he does not seem to have had a musical ear. He thought that he would have recognised the hymn if he had heard it. After his extensive research, he knew of only two survivors whose names were cited by newspapers as saying that the band played *Nearer, My God, to Thee*. All those to whom Gracie spoke personally after the tragedy stated that the hymn was *not* played. However, he only spoke to American passengers (not English or crew) as he did not travel back to England before his death. Peter Daly and Dick Williams, both on board till the last, only remembered cheerful music.

Violet Jessop, a stewardess aboard the *Titanic*, whose very readable memoirs were published posthumously, stated that she heard the band play *Nearer, My God, to Thee* as she was waiting to board a lifeboat. This may be the case, but, if she did hear it, then it was not the *final* piece of music, because the boats had all left when the last piece was played.

Mrs W.J. Doulton, whose husband was lost, had this to say, 'We rowed frantically away from the *Titanic* and were tied to four other boats. I arose and saw the ship sinking. The band was playing *Nearer, My God, to Thee*.'

Miss Gertrude Jean Hippach of Chicago, interviewed on landing in New York, said, 'To the last those poor musicians stood there, playing *Nearer, My God, to Thee*.' At this point in the interview, the girl's voice trembled and stopped.

Charlotte Collyer from Second Class, whose husband was lost, described the ship's final moments from a lifeboat, which was half a mile away:

> No sound reached us except the music of the band, which I seemed, strange to say, to be aware of for the first time. Oh, those brave musicians! How wonderful they were! They were playing lively tunes,

THE "TITANIC" DISASTER.

HEROIC BANDSMEN.

The survivors all say that as the boats were hurrying away from the wreck the Marine Band did its best to cheer up the waning hopes of the passengers. One or two airs were struck up. It was a spectacle which no one will ever forget.

"Suddenly the band stopped; the leader moved his baton, and in slow, solemn tones the air 'Nearer, my God, to Thee' was wafted across the water to our ears. The band played the hymn continuously until their instruments were choked off by the swirling water that closed about their heads as they went to a hero's grave."

By courtesy of the Musicians' Union.

rag-time, and they kept it up to the very end. Only the engulfing ocean had power to drown them into silence ... The band was playing *Nearer, My God, to Thee*; I could hear it distinctly. The end was very close.

Walter Lord, who wrote the book *A Night To Remember*, was eager to get details right. *Titanic* enthusiasts are indebted to him, as, after

One of a set of six postcards issued by the Holmfirth publisher, Bamforth, of the ship sinking. These 'song' cards were very popular at the time.

Nearer, My God, to Thee.

There let my way appear,
Steps unto heaven,
All that Thou sendest me
In mercy given,
Angels to beckon me,
Nearer, my God, to Thee,
Nearer to Thee,

talking to about sixty survivors, he managed to establish a timeline for events on the night in question. He wrote a letter to Colne Library, dated 19 June 1955, from his New York home, to ask for any information regarding the music that was played at the end. He wrote, 'Mr Hartley was a heroic man and I would like to do him justice.' In the famous film based on the book, what we hear at the end is *Nearer, My God, to Thee*. In his book, however, he gives a great deal of credence to the testimony of Harold Bride, who, as a wireless operator, was trained to listen carefully and report accurately.

So, what had Harold Bride heard? In an interview given in New York before he disembarked from the *Carpathia*, he stated quite categorically that he had heard *Autumn*. However, *Autumn* meant different things to different people. *Autumn* was not a hymn in itself:

Amalgamated Musicians' Union Monthly Report and Supplement.

General Office: 135, Moss Lane East, Manchester.

Telegraphic Address:
"AMUSE, Manchester."

Telephone
"Manchester, 5489."

No. 156.]   September, 1912.

CLARINET PLAYERS, send your Sick Instruments to the Doctor—H. MOON, MAKER and SPECIALIST in Clarinet Mouthpieces.

—o—

THE MIDDLESBROUGH B.S. is pleased to report the fact that this branch has now over 100 members, also wishes to draw particular attention to those members who are gradually dropping in arrears since the introduction of Funeral Levies, to make a special effort to clear their card on September meeting night.

—o—

OLDHAM BRANCH decided at their August meeting to hold their September Meeting on the Second Sunday (September 8th), owing to the First Sunday falling on Oldham Wakes Holidays. Members please note. Also any member wishing to see the Disengaged List may do so every Friday, at the Clubhouse, Dog and Duck Hotel, St. Domingo Street, on producing their contribution card.

—o—

Will members please note that to have their names on the weekly disengaged list, they must send through their Branch Secretaries.

—o—

HUDDERSFIELD BRANCH MEETING for September will be held on the 8th, on account of the week's holiday. All members are particularly requested to come to the meeting, as matters of great import to musicians are taking place.

—o—

STOCKPORT BRANCH.—Will all the members please note that the next General Meeting falls on the 8th of September, when everyone is earnestly requested to attend, as there is some important business to transact. This month being the end of the quarter, contribution cards will be required for audit. Before bringing, or

sending them, will all members in arrears kindly read and inwardly digest the Rule at the bottom of their card. Once more I wish to thank all those who so heartily responded to my last appeal for a reduction of the arrears; the response exceeded my expectations.

—o—

SPECIAL NOTICE.

Messrs. C. W. & F, N. Black have, we understand, given our members the choice between leaving the Union and leaving their service on the liners. Those members who are loyal have nothing to fear. The Union will support any member who is victimised. In the meantime, members are warned against playing for Messrs. Black until they pay the proper rate, £7 per month. It may be necessary to warn members against playing for them at all, no matter what the price, if they decline to come to terms with the Union. Members having any information to give that will be useful in this campaign should write the General Secretary.

—o—

A. M. U. CLUB, LIVERPOOL. A General Meeting of members will take place on Sunday evening, September 1st, to discuss a scheme of celebrating the first anniversary of the opening. It is suggested that a supper and smoker be held the first Sunday in October. Come to the meeting and decide what shall be done.

—o—

WILL LIVERPOOL MEMBERS please note next General Meeting will be held at Club, on 15th September, at 7 p.m. Very important business to be discussed.

From the September 1912 issue of the *Amalgamated Musicians' Union Journal and Report*. The union continued to have problems with the music agents for the shipping lines. (Courtesy of the Musicians' Union)

it was a tune, and was used for the Episcopalian hymn *God of Mercy and Compassion*. In the United States, it was used as a recessional.[3] The tune *Autumn* was also used for the hymn *Guide Me, O Thou Great Redeemer*, which, in this country, is usually sung to the tune *Cwm Rhondda*.

Hymnologists explain that, both in Great Britain and the United States, hymns are known by their first line, not the tune they are sung to, for example, *Amazing Grace*, or *I Vow to Thee, My Country* (not *Jupiter*).[4] If Harold Bride had been talking about a hymn, he would have referred to it as *God of Mercy and Compassion*, not *Autumn*. It is highly unlikely that he would even have known what the actual hymn tune was called.

Songe d'Automne appeared as song No.137 on page four of the White Star Line Music Book, possibly the last piece of music played on the fateful night.

127	Vision of Salome	...	...	...	Joyce
128	Remembrance	...	...	...	"
129	Beautiful Spring	...	...	...	Lincke
130	Wedding Dance	...	...	...	"
131	Comédie d'Amour	...	...	...	G. Colin
132	Valse Septembre	...	...	...	F. Godwin
133	Mondaine	...	...	...	Bosc
134	Rêve d'Artiste	...	...	...	"
135	Swing Song	...	...	...	Hollaender
136	Sphinx	...	...	...	Popy
137	Songe d'Automne	...	...	...	Joyce
138	La Lettre de Manon	...	...	...	Giliet
139	Verschmähte Liebe	...	...	...	P. Lincke
140	Lysistrata	...	...	...	"
141	Luna	...	...	...	"
142	L'Heure Suprême	...	...	...	A. Lotter
143	Rouge et Noir	...	...	...	"
144	Sans-Souci	...	...	...	Von Blon
145	Sizilietta	...	...	...	"
146	Gold and Silver	...	...	...	Lehar
147	A Waltz Dream	...	...	...	O. Strauss
148	The Merry Widow	...	...	...	Lehar

Gung'l Waltzes,
Strauss Waltzes,
Waldteufel Walzes.

What Harold Bride was probably referring to was *Songe d'Automne*, (meaning 'Autumn Dream'), a popular waltz by Archibald Joyce and a great hit in 1912. Because of the French title, this piece of music was usually referred to simply as *Autumn*.

Let us return to Mrs A.A. Dick, who originated the assertion that the band played *Nearer, My God, to Thee*. Although the people in the boats definitely heard the music as it wafted over the sea, Mrs Dick was in boat No.3, a quarter of a mile from the sinking vessel. Walter Lord, for one, doubts that she can have heard clearly enough. Perhaps Mrs Dick was thinking of another tragedy at sea, when the steamship *Valencia* foundered off the coast of British Columbia in 1905. The survivors had been discovered singing *Nearer, My God, to Thee* by a surfboat that came to the rescue. In addition the title of the hymn had allegedly been the last words of the assassinated President McKinley.

Furthermore, an American and a British passenger could not possibly agree that they had heard the same hymn that night, the reason for this being that there were several settings for the hymn, the words of which were written by Sarah Flower Adams. In England, the hymn is generally sung to the tune called *Horbury*, composed by John Bacchus Dykes. This is the setting used in the film *A Night to Remember*. On the other hand, the Methodists prefer the setting called *Propior Deo* by Arthur Sullivan. This is the tune that, as a Methodist, Wallace Hartley favoured, the tune that was played at his funeral. The notes of the Sullivan tune are inscribed on Wallace Hartley's gravestone. But, if Wallace Hartley had played this tune on the fateful night, would Archibald Gracie and the other American passengers have recognised it as the hymn in question? Definitely not, because, in the United States, the setting used is the wistful tune called *Bethany* by Dr Lowell Mason. This was the setting chosen by James Cameron for his film *Titanic*.[5] It has been suggested that Wallace Hartley may have chosen this setting because of the large numbers of American passengers on board.

In spite of Wallace Hartley's words to his friend Ellwand Moody, to the effect that, if he found himself on a sinking ship, he would play *Nearer, My God, to Thee*, he allegedly said to a journalist in 1911, prior to a voyage:

I've always felt that, when men are called to face death suddenly, music is far more effective in cheering them on than

all the firearms in creation. Should an accident befall my ship, I
know that every one of the men would stick with me, and play
until the waters engulfed us… lively music, of course. None
of your hymns, although I love them dearly. My favourite is
Nearer, My God, to Thee, but I'm keeping that one reserved
for my funeral.[6]

When Ellwand Moody was asked if he believed the report that
Nearer, My God, to Thee was played as the final piece of music, he had
this to say: 'If any other hymn tune had been mentioned … I should
have had my doubts about it … Knowing so well the kind of man he
was, I certainly believe that the story is true.'

Fred G. Vallance, of Detroit, Michigan, who was bandmaster on the
Cunarder *Laconia* in 1912, said that musicians working on ships at the
time were of the opinion that *Songe d'Automne* was the last piece of
music played on the fateful night. Once, when Vallance was playing
Songe d'Automne on board, a steward, who was a *Titanic* survivor, said it
was unlucky. Vallance explained that the musicians were playing in the
dark, on a sloping deck, without sheet music, so it would have to be
something that they all knew.[7] (The tune *Autumn* was more difficult
to play than other tunes suggested, and it was also a rather robust tune,
not in keeping with events.) A most important factor in determining
what was played last is the fact that *Songe d'Automne* was in the White
Star Song Book, No. 137, so all members of the band were obliged to
know it by heart. All Wallace Hartley would have to do was announce
the number and the musicians would immediately begin to play.

Songe d'Automne was popular in London, but not known in the
States. Therefore, whereas Harold Bride would easily have recognised
the tune (and he was near the band on deck when they started to
play), the American passengers would not know the tune at all, and
may have fancied that they heard the *Bethany* setting.

Songe d'Automne consists of an introduction (andante moderato),
followed by two alternating themes, played as a waltz (tempo di
valse). The two themes are quite different in character, and create
completely different moods, the opening one being haunting in
quality, the other quite lively. A notable difference between the pieces
mentioned, therefore, was that the hymns were obviously played to
a different tempo. This would explain why some heard only lively
music to the end, but others were more aware of the actual tune, but
everybody seemed to hear something different.

The power of hymns to inspire people cannot be underestimated. W.T. Stead, the famous journalist who perished in the disaster, wrote an article in 1897 entitled 'Hymns that have helped', in which he explains that hymns can 'renew our strength and dispel our fears'. D.H. Lawrence, too, was aware that hymns work on a level above criticism and analysis. Most people *wanted* the last piece of music to be a hymn as a source of inspiration and comfort.

To conclude, in the first few days after the disaster, the hymn had entered into the public consciousness, and, once there, it became 'fact', and could not be erased.

Certainly, the vast majority of people in the boats that night could hear the strains of the band until shortly before she took her final plunge. What they actually heard is a matter of opinion.

Many survivors were not sure what they heard. Some, having heard a vaguely familiar tune, and having heard the title *Nearer, My God, to Thee* bandied about, may have convinced themselves that it was indeed the hymn that they had heard. This may have been the case with Violet Jessop, the stewardess.

But it was the public at large, safely tucked up in bed during the tragedy, who adopted the hymn, rather than the survivors. There was *Titanic* fervour at the time that was almost verging on mass hysteria, and people were hungry for heroic deeds. With all due respect to the late Princess Diana, the effect can be likened to the appeal of *Candle in the Wind*. In fact, had there been a Hit Parade in 1912, sales of the hymn would probably have beaten all previous records, and it would have stayed in the No.1 position for weeks.

Personally, I think that, all things considered, it was probably *Songe d'Automne* that was the last piece of music to be played, the two most convincing pieces of evidence being that it was heard by Harold Bride, the most reliable witness and closest to where the musicians were standing, and secondly, it was in the White Star Line Song Book, so it could be played without hesitation by all the bandsmen.

However, in the words of Walter Lord, 'Whatever they played, they achieved immortality. The bravery of these men, trying to bring hope and comfort to others without a thought for their own safety.'

The public at large wanted the hymn to be the last piece of music played, and fervently believed that this was so. It is no longer a question of facts, but of a *legend*. The legend has lasted for 100 years. So be it.

NEARER MY GOD TO THEE!

Nearer, my God, to Thee, Nearer to Thee

E'en though it be a cross That raiseth me,

Still all my song shall be, Nearer, my God, to Thee, Nearer to Thee.

Though like the wanderer,
The sun gone down,
Darkness comes over me,
My rest a stone
Yet in my dreams I'd be
Nearer, my God, to Thee,
Nearer to Thee.

There let my way appear
Steps unto Heav'n,
All that Thou sendest me
In mercy given,
Angels to beckon me
Nearer, my God, to Thee,
Nearer to Thee.

Then, with my waking thoughts
Bright with Thy praise,
Out of my stony griefs
Beth-el I'll raise;
So by my woes to be
Nearer, my God, to Thee,
Nearer to Thee.

**Hymn played by Bandsmen of the S.S. "TITANIC" as she sank to
her doom, 15th April, 1912.**

The music and lyrics of *Nearer, My God, to Thee*. (Darran Ward)

Endnotes

1   Only the stringed instruments could be played in the circumstances. The pianists probably stayed with the other bandsmen all night. They, too, were lost along with the others.

2   The identity of the survivor who gave the interview is unknown.

3   A recessional is a hymn sung as the clergy and choir leave the church.

4   'Jupiter' is a movement from the *Planet Suite* by Holst and is used as the music for the hymn *I Vow to Thee, My Country*.

5   Cameron, who had researched the events of the sinking meticulously, was aware of the assertions that *Songe d'Automne* was the music played at the end, but he also knew that *Nearer, My God, to Thee* was Wallace Hartley's favourite hymn. He deliberately chose the hymn for his film and was undoubtedly aware of the poignancy it created; the whole sequence when the hymn was being played was quite beautiful. The music was arranged for the film by Jonathan Evans-Jones, who played Wallace Hartley in the film. A musician by profession, this was his first film role, and he bore a resemblance to the real Wallace.

6   This alleged report appeared on a *Titanic* website, but there is no mention of which newspaper the article appeared in. I have not seen the article in question, and, so far, I have not seen it mentioned in any other literature surrounding the tragedy.

7   No sheet music was allowed. The musicians had to play from memory.

9

Tributes and Memorials

Even before Wallace Hartley's body had been recovered from the North Atlantic, people up and down the country were rallying and organising themselves into action.

Tributes poured in from all over the world, praising the bravery of the bandsmen. The Hartley family received several hundred letters. The following are excerpts which, as well as remarking on the heroism of the musician, also give an insight into the character of the man:

'Our short lives will soon be over, and we shall soon be forgotten, but your son has emblazoned his name on the roll of honour, and will be spoken of and referred to by generations unborn.'

'I always held him in the highest esteem as one of the most kind and genial musicians it was ever my pleasure to meet, and consider him not only a loss to you, but to the musical world.'

'He was a quiet, genuine, unassuming lad, and every ounce a hero. I feel proud to have known him. The orchestra of the *Titanic* will go down in history as the noblest band on record.'

'Poor Wallace – a grand lad and a true friend. We cannot think of him without shedding bitter tears.'

'A splendid musician he was,' said one of his former colleagues from Leeds, 'and a better fellow you could not meet in a day's march. He was one of the best.'

'Your son was one of the nicest and most gentlemanly lads I ever met.'

'My friendship with Wallace was an old one … I know that you have lost a noble son. He was always a noble, manly fellow, and incapable of anything mean. His life was like his death – unselfish.'

'So much was his ability appreciated, also his charming disposition, that many in this little town of ours today endeavour to share with you in your grief.' – Gravesend.

'He gave me many a bright and encouraging smile when he saw I was down-hearted…You have the deepest sympathy of all those who met him at Collinson's Café, Leeds, especially the staff.'

'I always had the highest opinion of his character and common-sense. He was always solid and thoughtful.'

'We liked him very much, as, indeed, everyone must who knew him. We feel it a privilege to have known Wallace in his early manhood.'

One newspaper printed the headline: GREATEST HERO OF THE *TITANIC*.

A journalist writing in the *Leeds Mercury* had this to say: 'The part played by the orchestra on board the *Titanic* in the last dreadful moments will rank among the noblest in the annals of heroism at sea.'

Sir Arthur Conan Doyle, in reply to a critical article by George Bernard Shaw, referred to 'the beautiful incident of the band'.

Several people have voiced the opinion that one of the most striking images of the disaster that has imprinted itself on their minds is the one of the band playing as the ship sank. Among these is Harold Bride, the wireless operator, who gave an interview for the *New York Times* on 19 April, before disembarking from the *Carpathia*: 'The way the band played was a noble thing … How they ever did it I cannot imagine. That [and the way his colleague, Jack Phillips, carried on working] are the two things that stand out in my mind over all the rest.'

Elias Canetti was a child at the time of the disaster, but he vividly remembers hearing people talking about it in hushed tones. In his memoirs, he writes: 'The thing that had the biggest impact on me was the band that kept playing as the ship sank.'

A journalist: 'Few things in the last hours strike the imagination like the record of the bandsmen playing to the end.'

At the 17th Annual Convention of the American Federation of Musicians, held on 30 May 1912, the following resolutions were offered:

Whereas, among the many acts of individual bravery credited to those who perished in the disaster, none stand out in bolder relief than the heroic conduct of Wallace Hartley, John Hume, Percy C. Taylor, J. Wesley Woodward, J.F.C. Clarke, Georges Krins, W.T. Brailey and Roger Bricoux, composing the ship's orchestra, who in the darkness and terror of that awful tragedy, and in the face of certain death for themselves, remained at the post of duty, unswerving to the last, and by playing, cheered and comforted their fellow unfortunates until the icy waves of the Atlantic engulfed all and for ever stilled the harmony of their instruments.

They extended their condolences to the families of the dead musicians, after which a memorial service was held, during which Mrs A.A. Covalt sang *Nearer, My God, to Thee*.

On Saturday evening, just a few days after the sinking of the *Titanic*, there was a moving incident at Collinson's Café in Leeds, where Wallace Hartley had led the orchestra for some time, and whose colleagues had given him an engraved silver match-box holder when he left. The fashionable café was full of prominent citizens of Leeds, and was buzzing with conversation. The members of the orchestra, joined by other musician friends of Wallace's, began to play *Nearer, My God, to Thee*. Conversation suddenly stopped, and everyone in the café stood in silence while the hymn was played.

On Sunday 21 April, several memorial services were held for Wallace Hartley. At the Bethel Independent Methodist Chapel in Colne, where his funeral service would take place a few weeks later, a service was held for a large congregation, among whom were many of Wallace's relatives. During the service, the now famous hymn was sung, and everyone was deeply affected. 'Many people burst into tears, and there was scarcely a dry eye in the whole building.' Mr Pickles Riley, who was a member of the old choir and helped Wallace with his playing, seconded the resolution, but was so deeply moved he could scarcely speak and almost broke down.

On the evening of the same day, a sacred concert was held in the Grand Pavilion on the Royal Prince's Parade in Bridlington.[1] Some of the bandsmen that Wallace had played with early in his career were still in the Municipal Orchestra, including Mr Hemingway, whose son had been in the *Lusitania* band with Wallace. Herr Winternitz was no longer with the orchestra, which was conducted by Signor Scoma. The programme opened with Chopin's Funeral March 'in memory of Mr Wallace Hartley, the brave musical director of the *Titanic* orchestra, and formerly leader of the Parade Orchestra, and of all those who lost their lives in the terrible disaster.' The closing hymn was *Nearer, My God, to Thee*, and the audience, described as 'an unusually saddened company,' rose to join in the singing.

In Dewsbury, a memorial service was held at St Mark's Church, which stood on the main road into the town from Halifax, at the corner of West Park Street, where the Hartley family lived.

The following day, a meeting was held in Leeds, attended by all the *chefs d'orchestre* in the city. The musicians of Leeds, many of whom were friends of Wallace Hartley and also of Roger Bricoux, were determined that a permanent memorial should be provided in remembrance of Wallace Hartley and his fellow musicians. To fund this project, a large concert was planned for the following Sunday. The selection of vocalists and the organisation of the joint orchestras were enthusiastically undertaken by the members of a sub-committee, which comprised the city organist, the manager of the Leeds Empire, conductors of the Empire, Grand Theatre and Hippodrome bands, and a representative of the Theatre Royal.

The honorary secretary of the committee which had been formed to raise money for the memorial was the manager of Collinson's Café, Mr A. Drudie. He and Wallace Hartley had been 'close friends'. Subscriptions were being collected at the premises on King Edward Street.

The concert in Leeds duly took place on Sunday 28 April at the Theatre Royal, the patron being the Lord Mayor.[2] The house was packed to overflowing long before the starting time, and hundreds were turned away disappointed. Many local musicians were giving their services in support of the memorial fund. The orchestra of eighty was composed mainly of musicians from Leeds, and was conducted in turn by several conductors from theatres in the city. When one of the soloists, Miss Lily Jeffreys, sang Mendelssohn's *Be Thou Faithful unto Death*, the cello obbligato was played by Ellwand Moody, Wallace Hartley's friend from the *Mauretania* and himself a resident of Leeds. The famous hymn, now inextricably linked to the musicians of the *Titanic*, was also played during the course of the evening. A silver collection took place in aid of the memorial fund, and a total of £101 was collected.

With the proceeds, the musicians of Leeds commissioned a painting by the artist F. Cayley-Robinson. Entitled *The Outward Bound*, it shows the *Titanic* setting sail in the distance, viewed by a wistful observer from a small sailing boat in the foreground. The painting was presented to the City Art Gallery, and an unveiling ceremony was held on 23 December. The painting was formerly on display in the main entrance hall of the Gallery.

At the Kursaal in Harrogate, the concert of Wednesday 24 April had an additional item on the programme; the Municipal Orchestra played Sullivan's *In Memoriam* overture 'in memory of those who lost their lives in the *Titanic* disaster'. The *Harrogate Advertiser* went on to explain, 'The leader of the saloon orchestra, Mr Hartley, was at one time a member of the Kursaal orchestra, and, in fact, is affectionately remembered by his old confreres; therefore the tribute had a strong local application.'

In Slaithwaite, just outside Huddersfield, the Philharmonic Society passed a resolution of sympathy with the relatives of the late Wallace Hartley. Their conductor, Mr Arthur Armitage, had played alongside Wallace in the violin section of the Huddersfield Philharmonic Orchestra.

The people of Colne had also been busy. On 26 April, *The Times* newspaper (the national daily newspaper, *not* the *Colne Times*), along with coverage of the disaster, ran a short article:

> A sub-committee of the Colne Town Council has decided to appeal for £500 for the purpose of erecting a memorial to Mr Wallace Hartley, the conductor of the Titanic's band, who lost his life in the disaster. Mr Hartley was a native of Colne.

In May, the borough council of Colne, led by the Mayor, Mr Turner Hartley, published a flier announcing their decision. Under the heading WALLACE HARTLEY MEMORIAL FUND, the announcement ran thus:

> As Mayor of the Borough, I have been requested to open a Fund for the erection of a Memorial, of a substantial and permanent character, to the memory of the late Mr Wallace Hartley, Bandmaster on the Titanic, who was a native of the Borough and for many years a member of the Colne Orchestral Society, and who, whilst leading the ship's orchestra, so heroically lost his life on the ill-fated vessel on the 15th April, 1912 [...] I am further desired to state, for the information of the public, that it has been deemed most fitting that a Water Fountain or other suitable Memorial should be erected in front of the Municipal Hall or in the Library Grounds [...]

Another musical tribute was paid by Miss Edna Lyall, a personal acquaintance of Wallace Hartley, who sang *Nearer, My God, to Thee* at the London Coliseum on 1 May.

A concert, expressly organised to raise funds for a memorial, was held in Dewsbury on Sunday 12 May. The initiative was taken by the Dewsbury Permanent Orchestra. Also taking part were the Dewsbury Military Band along with various professional and amateur musicians who offered their services, the augmented orchestra eventually comprising approximately seventy musicians. The concert was held at the Victoria Hall, in the Town Hall building, under the patronage of Mr Walter Runciman MP, and the Mayor and Mayoress of Dewsbury. Wallace Hartley's father and one of his sisters were present. The concert opened with Sullivan's setting of *Nearer, My God, to Thee*, followed by a varied programme. The vocalists were Mr Harry Ward Kemp and Miss Mabel Porritt. One of the great features of the concert was a piece played on the cello by Wallace's friend, Ellwand Moody.

In order to augment the funds raised from the concert, an appeal was made to various gentlemen in the Dewsbury district for donations, and a Mr Frank Gibson, of Hope Street, was authorised to receive subscriptions. Because of the numbers who had not been able to gain admission to the concert, a second concert was held the following Sunday, albeit with a far smaller audience. The programme was virtually the same, one notable absentee being Ellwand Moody.

The original purpose of the Dewsbury concerts had been the 'erection of some public memorial' to perpetuate the memory of the *Titanic*'s orchestra. However, there is no memorial in the centre of the town, the only memorial in existence being a bronze plaque that was placed on a wall in St Mark's Church.[3] On the plaque, along with the names of the bandsmen, which are encircled with laurel wreath are the words:

> GREATER LOVE HATH NO MAN THAN
> THIS, THAT HE LAY DOWN HIS LIFE
> FOR HIS FRIENDS.

On 19 May, the same Sunday evening as the second Dewsbury concert, another event was held at the Palace Theatre, Manchester, this one having been arranged by the Amalgamated Musicians' Union. During the concert, an actor recited a poem he had written about the role of the *Titanic* musicians, from which this is an extract:

Picture that gallant little band
At dead of night quietly taking their stand,
And at their brave leader Hartley's command
Playing their dirge to another land.

Other branches of the Amalgamated Musicians' Union organised concerts, including Bury, Ashton and Newcastle. A number of letters praising the actions of the band were received by the Musicians' Union. The Union also produced a broadsheet to raise money for the families of the deceased bandsmen: in the space of one month, 80,000 copies were sold.

Meanwhile, money was pouring into the memorial fund in Colne. There was some disagreement, however, as to the form the memorial should take. A drinking fountain had been suggested, but objections were raised. A regular contributor to the *Colne and Nelson Times*, writing under the pseudonymn Fran-Du-Col, expressed his misgivings regarding the drinking fountain: 'Surely there has been enough water in this sad affair without introducing any more … I should like to see a life-size bronze statue, showing the brave lad with baton in hand, upraised, as if conducting his beloved orchestra.'

In stark contrast to the generosity of so many was the behaviour of the White Star Line towards the bereaved families, who sought compensation under the Workmen's Compensation Act. Since the bandsmen had boarded as passengers, not crew, the shipping line said that they were not responsible, that the employers were actually the music agents in Liverpool. C.W. and F.N. Black told the families to contact the insurance agents, who, in turn, said that the bandsmen were not workmen as such, but were independent contractors. The families sued the Black brothers, the notice of claim being sent on 5 June, and the case came up before the Liverpool County Court judge in November 1912. It is not known whether the Hartley family was involved. The judge was sympathetic, but was obliged to rule against the plaintiffs, adding: 'I wish to add this observation. Although I have felt compelled to hold that the Workmen's Compensation Act does not apply to the bandsmen, yet I cannot forget that these brave men met their death while performing an act which was of the greatest service in assisting to maintain discipline and avert panic.' Finally, the *Titanic* Relief Fund recognised the musicians as crewmembers and awarded the families an undisclosed sum of money.

CITY ART GALLERY, LEEDS.

WALLACE HARTLEY MEMORIAL.

The Chairman (Alderman A. W. WILLEY) and Committee have the pleasure to invite

Koo W Hand ....and friend

to the UNVEILING of "THE OUTWARD BOUND," by F. Cayley Robinson, presented by the Musicians of Leeds to the City Art Gallery to commemorate the heroism of WALLACE HARTLEY, late of Leeds, Bandmaster of the S.S. Titanic.

Monday, December 23rd, at 4 p.m.

R.S.V.P.

LIGHT REFRESHMENTS.   FRANK RUTTER, Curator.

An invite to the unveiling of F. Cayley-Robinson's painting at Leeds City Art Gallery. (By courtesy of Leeds Library & Information Services)

The family of violinist Jock Hume were also treated rather shabbily by the Black brothers. Two weeks after the disaster, they received a letter asking for a paltry sum for various items connected with uniform, such as lapel badges.

It will be remembered that Wallace's violin, which had been strapped to his body when he was recovered, but would have had to be removed for the embalming process, was forwarded to the White Star offices in New York, after which the belief is that it was returned to Wallace's fiancée. In 1912, a violin was made in Colne to commemorate Wallace Hartley. It is now traditionally presented to the leader of the Burnley Youth Orchestra.

In Southampton, a memorial to the musicians was unveiled in April 1913 by the Sheriff Councillor in the library building. During the Second World War, the library and the monument were destroyed. A replica was erected at the Municipal Mutual building, and was unveiled in 1990. Present at the unveiling ceremony were *Titanic* survivors, including Eva Hart, Bertram Dean and his sister

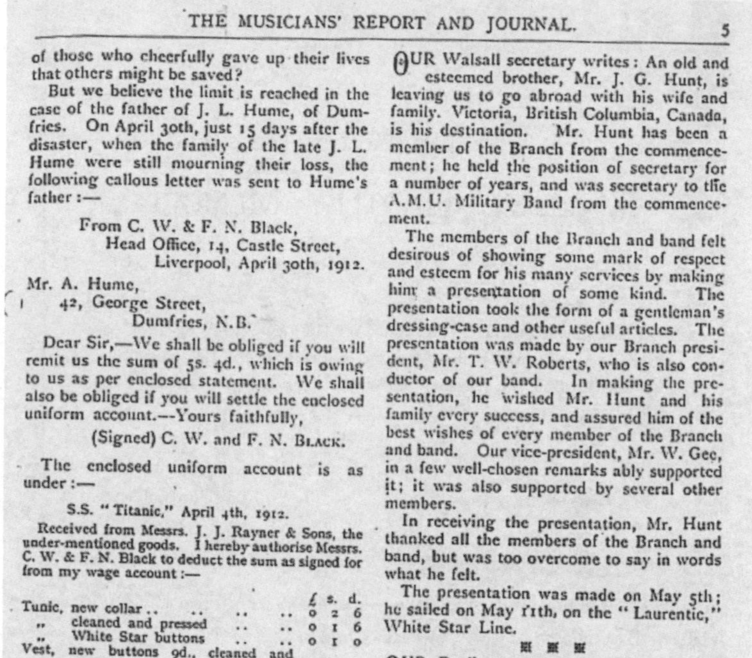

THE MUSICIANS' REPORT AND JOURNAL. 5

of those who cheerfully gave up their lives that others might be saved?

But we believe the limit is reached in the case of the father of J. L. Hume, of Dumfries. On April 30th, just 15 days after the disaster, when the family of the late J. L. Hume were still mourning their loss, the following callous letter was sent to Hume's father:—

From C. W. & F. N. Black,
Head Office, 14, Castle Street,
Liverpool, April 30th, 1912.

Mr. A. Hume,
42, George Street,
Dumfries, N.B.

Dear Sir,—We shall be obliged if you will remit us the sum of 5s. 4d., which is owing to us as per enclosed statement. We shall also be obliged if you will settle the enclosed uniform account.—Yours faithfully,

(Signed) C. W. and F. N. Black.

The enclosed uniform account is as under:—

S.S. "Titanic," April 4th, 1912.

Received from Messrs. J. J. Rayner & Sons, the under-mentioned goods. I hereby authorise Messrs. C. W. & F. N. Black to deduct the sum as signed for from my wage account:—

	£	s.	d.
Tunic, new collar	0	2	6
" cleaned and pressed	0	1	6
" White Star buttons	0	1	0
Vest, new buttons 9d., cleaned and pressed 6d.	0	1	3
Trousers cleaned and pressed	0	1	0
Lyre, small	0	2	0
	£0	9	3

Signed John Hume.
Witness S. B. Yeomans.

Notice.—Please see that your goods correspond with this invoice.

Comment would be superfluous!

❖ ❖ ❖

On April 19th, Mr. H. Payne, late musical director, Hippodrome, Ipswich, sailed for Canada to take up an appointment at Winnipeg. Before leaving, Mr. H. Payne was presented by the management, orchestra, and staff with a watch and chain, as a mark of esteem and appreciation of his services as musical director, and with the hearty good wishes of all for his success in the land of his adoption.

Our Walsall secretary writes: An old and esteemed brother, Mr. J. G. Hunt, is leaving us to go abroad with his wife and family. Victoria, British Columbia, Canada, is his destination. Mr. Hunt has been a member of the Branch from the commencement; he held the position of secretary for a number of years, and was secretary to the A.M.U. Military Band from the commencement.

The members of the Branch and band felt desirous of showing some mark of respect and esteem for his many services by making him a presentation of some kind. The presentation took the form of a gentleman's dressing-case and other useful articles. The presentation was made by our Branch president, Mr. T. W. Roberts, who is also conductor of our band. In making the presentation, he wished Mr. Hunt and his family every success, and assured him of the best wishes of every member of the Branch and band. Our vice-president, Mr. W. Gee, in a few well-chosen remarks ably supported it; it was also supported by several other members.

In receiving the presentation, Mr. Hunt thanked all the members of the Branch and band, but was too overcome to say in words what he felt.

The presentation was made on May 5th; he sailed on May 11th, on the "Laurentic," White Star Line.

❖ ❖ ❖

Our Darlington secretary writes: I am pleased to say that every member of the orchestras of the Theatre Royal and Hippodrome here are now members of the A.M.U.

❖ ❖ ❖

In the "Encore" of May 2nd, dealing with the current week's programme at the Kilburn Empire, the writer ascribes its success as largely due to "genial George Hatley who wags the stick, and has got round him one of the finest bands in London." They are all Union men there, and in that fact therein often lies the reason for smooth working and good playing. In addition to doing his best from his own standpoint, the true Union man does all he can to make his show a success, so that the Union may get credit from his performances. Instead of causing trouble, a Union orchestra very often prevents it, for while the Union man demands just and fair treatment for himself he also insists on others having it as well.

Report from the Musicians' Union magazine referring to the Black brothers' heavy-handed treatment of Jock Hume's family after the sinking. (By courtesy of the Musicians' Union)

Millvina, the youngest of all the *Titanic* survivors. At the time of the sinking she was only nine weeks old.

The tribute which was conspicuous by its absence was the one that should have come from the Savage Club of Leeds.[4] The *Leeds Mercury* reported that the Braves were lamenting the loss of a pleasant companion who often contributed to the harmony of their evenings. However, the club members held meetings on 6 and 17 June 1912 to discuss a forthcoming concert, but there was no mention of Wallace Hartley in the minutes. The Savage Club disbanded shortly after, their last meeting being on 12 July. Once again, there was no mention of the dead musicians, nor any evidence that the Savage Club had contributed in any way to the fundraising carried out for a Leeds memorial.

The greatest tribute paid to Wallace Hartley and the *Titanic*'s orchestra was a benefit concert held at the Royal Albert Hall on Friday 24 May, in the afternoon. The largest orchestra ever assembled, comprising seven of the world's leading orchestras, gathered to play the bandsmen's requiem. The huge orchestra, comprising 500 musicians, was conducted by the leading conductors of the day, including Sir Henry Wood, Thomas Beecham and Sir Edward Elgar. In the audience were two ladies who had survived the disaster, and Princess Henry of Battenberg was in the royal box.

The first item on the programme was Chopin's *Marche Funebre*, played by the 500 standing musicians. Next came Sullivan's overture *In Memoriam*. Elgar conducted his work *Variations* to rapturous applause, and there followed excerpts from the third movement in Tchaikovsky's *Symphonie Pathétique*. The journalist reporting for the *Daily Sketch* had this to say:

> The supreme moment of the day came when Sir Henry Wood led the orchestra through the first eight bars of Dykes' version of Nearer, My God, to Thee, and then, turning to the audience, he conducted the singing to the end. Ten thousand people, whose minds were filled with thoughts of one of the greatest sea tragedies ever known, sang the hymn with deep feeling.

Funeral March	(Arranged by Sir Henry J. Wood)	Chopin
	(Conducted by Sir HENRY J. WOOD)	
Overture	'In Memoriam'	Sullivan
	(Conducted by Mr. Percy Pitt)	

Variations for Full Orchestra Op.36		Elgar
	(Conducted by Sir EDGAR ELGAR O.M.)	
Aria	'O Rest in the Lord' ('Elijah')	Mendelssohn
	Sung by Madame Ada Crossley	
	(Conducted by Mr. Percy Pitt)	
Third Movement (Scherzo) from Symphony No. 6,		Tchaikowsky
	in B minor ('Pathetic')	
	(Conducted by Mr. Landon Ronald)	

INTERVAL

Prelude	'Die Meistersinger'	Wagner
	(Conducted by Herr Mengelberg)	
Aria (for strings)		Bach
	(Conducted by Sir HENRY J. WOOD)	
'The Ride of the Valyries' ('Die Walküre)		Wagner
	(Conducted by Mr. Thomas BEECHAM)	
Vorspiel	'Lohengrin'	Wagner
	(Conducted by M. Fritz Ernaldy)	
Overture	'Tannhauser'	Wagner
	(Conducted by Herr Mengelberg)	
Hymn	'Nearer My God to Thee'	Dykes
	(Orchestrated by Sir Henry Wood)	
	(Conducted by Sir Henry Wood)	

GOD SAVE THE KING

Programme for the Titanic Band Memorial concert, held on 24 May at the Royal Albert Hall.

In Colne, the sum of £265 was eventually raised. Instead of the life-size statue suggested in the letter to the local newspaper, it was decided that a bronze bust on a pedestal would be more appropriate. The memorial was commissioned from the Bromsgrove Guild, Bromsgrove, Worcestershire, and executed under the supervision of the Borough Surveyor, Mr T.H. Hartley.

The memorial stands 10ft high from base to crown. At the base of the memorial are two granite steps, 5ft 6in square. The pedestal stands

6ft 6in high and is of Hopton Wood stone with an eggshell finish. Seated on the pedestal are two bronze statuettes, depicting Music and Valour. The bronze bust itself measures 2ft 6in and is reminiscent of those dedicated to great composers, with its noble, dignified air, showing every feature to its best advantage, and accentuating traits often associated with musicians, for example the rather long hair with its Romantic sweep. The handsome features, although somewhat enhanced, are instantly recognisable as those from a photograph in circulation at the time, and used by the Amalgamated Musicians' Union for their broadsheet.

The unveiling ceremony took place on Wednesday 17 February 1915. Albion Hartley travelled to Colne for the event. Also present were the Mayor, members of the Town Council and subscribers to the memorial. By the time of the unveiling, there was no shortage of British heroes, and in every edition of local newspapers, there were photographs of those who had lost their lives or had been maimed in the carnage of the First World War. The Mayor, who performed the ceremony, spoke of different kinds of heroism: the soldiers, who gave up their lives for King and country on the battlefield, and the bandsmen in mid-Atlantic, with no elements of pomp and circumstance, who thought of others rather than trying to save themselves. He did not think of Wallace Hartley as dead; the memory of his heroism was a constant inspiration.

The memorial stands in the grounds of what was the Carnegie Library, and, since its erection, a monument to those fallen in the two world wars has been erected a few yards away. On the front of the pedestal, in cast bronze letters, are the words:

WALLACE HARTLEY
Bandmaster of
The R.M.S. Titanic,
Who perished in
The foundering
Of that vessel,
April 15th, 1912.
Erected by voluntary
Contributions to com-
Memorate the heroism
Of a native of this
Town.

Endnotes

1 Not to be confused with the Floral Pavilion, this pavilion was built of wood in 1906 and stood just further along the Parade.

2 The Theatre Royal used to stand on Land's Lane at the intersection with King Charles' Croft. There is now a modern shopping development here. The Laura Ashley shop stands next to the site of the theatre.

3 St Mark's Church closed in 1998, and the plaque was removed to the diocesan headquarters at Wakefield. It will eventually be relocated to the heritage centre at the Minster, Dewsbury. At the time of writing, the plaque is still in storage in Wakefield.

4 Wallace Hartley's name does not appear in any of the Savage Club records, either the minutes of the meetings, the club address book or concert programmes. Because of this I have my doubts as to whether he was really a member. Perhaps the newspapers were making assumptions, as this is exactly the kind of club that Wallace would have belonged to, and I have no difficulty picturing him with the merry throng. Two other musicians by the name of Hartley joined the Club at this time: Lloyd, pianist (1908) and James, cellist (1910), so some confusion may have arisen. However, the timing of his supposed last concert is correct (1908), as his family left Leeds in that year. Another mystery.

Epilogue

A stone was erected over Wallace Hartley's grave. It is in the form of a draped, broken column, denoting a life cut short too soon. At the base there is a violin and the first few bars of Sullivan's setting for the hymn *Nearer, My God, to Thee*. Wallace's infant brothers were already buried in the grave, and the three sons have since been joined by their mother and father.

Albion Hartley retired in 1915 and, with his wife, Elizabeth, moved to the delightful spa town of Harrogate, where Wallace had played. Here they lived in Church Avenue, off Skipton Road, and here they both eventually died, Mrs Hartley in 1927, aged seventy-six, and her husband in 1934 at the age of eighty-three.

Maria Robinson and the remainder of her family moved out of the house in Boston Spa. Maria eventually withdrew to Bridlington, where she lived at 11 Marine Drive. Did she choose Bridlington because of its connections with Wallace? That question will never be answered.

Maria never married. She died on 28 June 1939, at the age of fifty-nine. Her sister, Margaret, was at her bedside.

Today, the Hartley grave is seldom without flowers. An American lady has left roses with pledges of undying love. A child has left a teddy bear brooch resting on the violin.

The cemetery in Colne has not changed since Wallace Hartley was laid to rest. The same atmosphere of serene tranquillity reigns here. The eye wanders across to the hill-side dotted with cattle.

… And overhead a lark sings.

Select Bibliography

Aylmer, Gerald (additional text by Janette McCutcheon), 2000, *RMS Mauretania: The Ship and Her Record*, Tempus Publishing

Beesley, Lawrence, 1912, *The Loss of SS Titanic*, London: William Heinemann

Behe, George, 1988, *Titanic: Psychic Forewarnings of a Tragedy*, Stephens

Bryceson, Dave (compiled by), 1997, *The Titanic Disaster: as reported in the British national press, April-July*, Stephens

Eaton, John P. and Charles A. Haas, 1996, *Titanic: Destination Disaster*, Sparkford, Somerset: Patrick Stephens

Geller, Judith B., 1998, *Women and Children First*, Stephens

Gibbs, Philip, 1985, *The Deathless Story of the Titanic*, London: Lloyds

Gracie, Archibald, 1913, *The Truth about the Titanic*, New York: Mitchell Kennerley

Harrison, Dorothy, *A History of Colne*

Jessop, Violet (edited by John Maxtone-Graham), 1998, *Titanic Survivor: The Memoirs of Violet Jessop, stewardess*, Sutton

Lightoller, Charles, 1935, *Titanic and Other Ships*, London: Nicholson and Watson

Lord, Walter, 1955, *A Night to Remember*, New York: Henry Holt

Lynch, Don and Ken Marschall, 1992, *Titanic: An Illustrated History*, London: Hodder & Stoughton

McCluskie, Tom, 1998, *Anatomy of the Titanic*, PRC

Quinn, Paul J., 1997, *Titanic at 2a.m.*, Fantail

The Cunard express liners Lusitania *and* Mauretania (compiled from *The Shipbuilder* periodical), 1970, Wellingborough: Patrick Stephens

Wade, Wyn Craig, 1980, *The Titanic, End of a Dream*, Weidenfeld

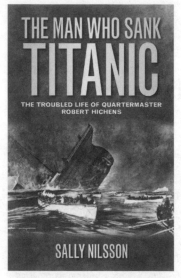

THE MAN WHO SANK TITANIC: THE TROUBLED LIFE OF QUARTMASTER ROBERT HICHENS

Sally Nilsson

Robert Hichens has gone down in history as the man who was given the famous order to steer the *Titanic* away from the iceberg and failed. Following this, his falling out with the 'Unsinkable Molly Brown' over the actions of the lifeboats saw him branded a coward and his name indelibly tarnished. With previously unpublished material from the Hichens family archives, Robert's great-granddaughter Sally Nilsson seeks to set the record straight and reveal the true character of the man her family knew.

978 0 7524 6071 0

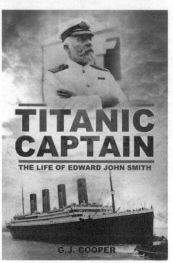

TITANIC CAPTAIN: THE LIFE OF EDWARD JOHN SMITH

G.J. Cooper

Commander Edward John Smith's career had been a remarkable example of how a man from a humble background could get far in the world. Born to a working-class family he went to sea at seventeen and by 1912 he was the White Star Line's senior commander. That year he was given command of the new RMS *Titanic* for her maiden voyage, but what should have been the crowning moment of a long career turned into a nightmare. This biography is packed full of detail and insight into the life of this legendary captain, who went down with his ship.

978 0 7524 6072 7

For the full Titanic experience visit The History Press website and follow the Titanic link. For stories and articles about Titanic, join us on Facebook.

www.thehistorypress.co.uk